**Prayer Artillery
Higher Levels of Prayer
For
End Time Strategic Warfare**

Myra D. Sampy

A Book Of Prayers

THANKS AND ACKNOWLEDGMENTS

To my Father God in heaven, the Lord and Savior Jesus Christ and the Holy Spirit I thank you for all the support, love and grace you have given me throughout the years! Nothing I do would be possible without the three of you. Thank you Lord Jesus for teaching my hands to war, and my fingers to fight.

~ Psalms 144:1   I love you Lord God forever and always ...

To my husband David Sampy, what an amazing support you are. You are absolutely one in a million. I love you tremendously...

Hugs and kisses to our children and grandchildren

Dear reader, I pray that this book will aid you and complement your prayer arsenal with the grace of the Lord Jesus Christ. I along with many of you have walked in and through many dark places as the Lord was teaching me how to wage an effective warfare through situations and circumstances that I faced using the word of God. These prayers are a result of many encounters and spiritual battles by which I saw the victory manifest through prayer and a consistent life of intercession and fellowship with the Lord Jesus Christ.

This book and those that will follow are related to my reality through experience. Remember we are destined to win triumphantly so continue to stand your ground in prayer for your life, your family, your friends, your community and country.

Prayer Artillery
Higher Levels of Prayer
For
End Time Strategic Warfare

Introduction

As a christian prayer must be our foundation, through praying we are given the opportunity to communicate with our heavenly Father Jehovah. The Lord tells us that if we ask anything in His name in accordance to His will He will answer John 14:13-14. With this scripture in mind we know He hears us we have surety that we can give Him our prayers and supplication Philippians 4:6-7.

Prayer Artillery Higher Levels of Prayer is written to be an added tool to combat in spiritual warfare. Using the word of God is a very effective weapon during prayer. Within this book there are many scriptures used in the form of prayers. It is important before beginning spiritual warfare to reflect on any areas that there may be a need for personal repentance. Here is a simple yet effective repentance prayer:

Prayer
Father God in heaven I confess any sin and acts I have committed knowingly and unknowingly. (*you speak out your actual sins*) I denounce any workings of darkness in my life, please forgive me my trespasses. Please close any doors that I have opened to Satan as a result of disobedience and rebellion against Your holy word. Father God wash me throughly with the blood of Your son Jesus Christ and cleanse me from all unrighteousness in the name of Jesus Christ.

1 John 1:9
If we confess our sins, he is faithful and just to forgive us our sins, and to cleanse us from all unrighteousness.

Topics

Prayer Artillery
Higher Levels of Prayer
For
End Time Strategic Warfare

Binding And Loosing
Children
Activating the Seven Spirits Of God
Covenants   Contracts
Angelic Assistance
Deliverance
Animalistic Spirits
Direction
Abominable Animals
Favor
Charismatic Witchcraft
Fear
Defeating Giants
Gates
Dismantling Demonic Confederacies
Government / Nations
Destruction
Healing
Devil (The)
Restoration
Queen Spirit
Vindication
Marine Spirit
Monitoring Spirits
Marriage
8 Prayer Watches
Marital Delay
Adultery
Spiritual Weapons
Spirit Of Sorcery and Witchcraft
Elevation
Barrenness

Chapter 1
Binding And Loosing
Prayer Artillery
Higher Levels of Prayer
For
End Time Strategic Warfare

Psalms 140:7
O God the Lord , the strength of my salvation, you
have covered my head in the day of battle.

Now that we have done that we are ready to engage in
spiritual warfare. We do not engage alone, we must ask the
Lord to cover our head on the day of battle. The strategy
belongs to the Lord God for he is a man of war and will defeat
His enemies.

Exodus 15:3
The Lord is a man of war: the Lord is his name.

Let's get started...
Engaging in spiritual warfare is not for the timid, shy or those
who have the opinion that it doesn't take all of that in their
mindset. It does not matter if we choose to engage or not WE
ARE IN A BATTLE we are in a constant fight according to
Epehsians 6:12 *For we wrestle not against flesh and blood,*
but against principalities, against powers, against the rulers
of the darkness of this world, against spiritual wickedness in
high places.

Furthermore, we are made aware that we have all power over darkness. Let's read what Luke 10:19 says, *Behold, I give unto you power to tread on serpents and scorpions, and over all the power of the enemy: and nothing shall by any means hurt you.*

The Lord has given us the confidence through His word we can trust and believe Him.

Many times believers are timid, fearful and unwilling to commit to spiritual engagement. Simply because they are not aware of who they are in Christ. Let me explain there are times we can see others moving into the things of God such as, preaching, praying and prophesying etc. And assume not to be as special or gifted etc.

However, these are special gifts but you must not undermine yourself, you must know your rank with God. And with that being said each believer has been given authority we must activate, demonstrate and manifest dominion.

There are two degrees of authority I would like to discuss *(Binding)* and *(Loosing)* you will see the two often mentioned throughout prayers within this book.

According to the Oxford Dictionary Bind is: *tie or fasten (something) tightly. Restrict or Curtail. Or a statutory constraint.* Loose is: *set free; release.*

Now that we know what it means to bind or loose we can understand what the Lord is speaking in Matthew 16:19 *And I will give unto thee the keys of the kingdom of heaven: and whatsoever thou shalt bind on earth shall be bound in heaven: and whatsoever thou shalt loose on earth shall be loosed in heaven.*

The Lord in this scripture gave Peter the keys to the Kingdom. The keys to the Kingdom is the authority to bind on earth and heaven, loose on earth and loose in heaven. We also see the Lord Jesus confirming the principle of binding and loosing in Matthew 18:18-19 ***Verily I say unto you, Whatsoever ye shall bind on earth shall be bound in heaven: and whatsoever ye shall loose on earth shall be loosed in heaven.***
Again I say unto you, That if two of you shall agree on earth as touching anything that they shall ask, it shall be done for them of my Father which is in heaven.

So when we bind the enemy we are asking for the immediate arrest or constraint against the activities being done or displayed. When we are asking for things to be loosed we are asking for the release of things that are bound against us.

Let's look and some simple examples:

Binding - I bind up the spirits of chaos, anger and strife.
Loosing - I Loose the peace of God.

Binding - I bind all demonic spiritual hindrances that would come against my peace today.
Loosing - I loose myself from any and all demonic bondage. I loose the liberty of the Lord Jesus Christ over myself today!

Are you ready to activate binding and loosing in your life?

I Bind:

_____

_____

_____

_____

_____

I Loose:

_____

_____

_____

_____

_____

Activating the
Seven Spirits of God

And the spirit of the LORD shall rest upon him, the spirit of wisdom and understanding, the spirit of counsel and might, the spirit of knowledge and of the fear of the LORD;

The Lord God has made so much available to believers through faith. There are seven Spirits of God in which I like to consider to be the core principles to our statement of faith. We must walk in wisdom and understanding. We must ask and seek... James 1:5 *(If any of you lack wisdom, let him ask of God, that giveth to all men liberally, and upbraideth not; and it shall be given him).* We must be willing to accept the counsel of God. Proverbs 11:14 *(Where no counsel is, the people fall: but in the multitude of counselors there is safety.)*

With that being said it brings us to the need for knowledge. We have all heard the famous statement that, "Knowledge is Power!" ~ Francis Bacon
Knowledge is certainly the principle thing we see here in Hosea. We also see within the same scripture verse that destruction follows a lack of knowledge. This is all so sad but knowledge can also be rejected.

Hosea 4:6 *(My people are destroyed for lack of knowledge: because thou hast rejected knowledge, I will also reject thee, that thou shalt be no priest to me: seeing thou hast forgotten the law of thy God, I will also forget thy children.)*
Remaining focused on the will of God will keep us wanting and inquiring more knowledge.

We should earnestly seek to walk in the fear of the Lord Proverbs 9:10 *(The fear of the LORD is the beginning of wisdom: and the knowledge of the holy is understanding.)*
Wow! Do you see the antidote? The fear of the Lord is the beginning, the basis for wisdom. And knowledge of the HOLY brings about understanding. This is what I call an awesome three for one!

Wisdom, Knowledge and Understanding

Prayer
Father in heaven let Your spirit of rest upon me as I engage in spiritual warfare. I receive the spirit of wisdom to strategize effective prayers and understanding to execute the declarations and decrees.

Holy Spirit I invite your counsel and direction, Father God I ask that You will clothe me with the spirit of might that I may raise an effective warfare.

Lord Jesus please give me hidden knowledge and divine insight into mysteries and revelation concerning the enemy of my soul in the name of Jesus Christ. I will walk firmly in the fear of the Lord.

Judges 14:6
And the Spirit of the LORD came mightily upon him, and he rent him as he would have rent a kid, and he had nothing in his hand: but he told not his father or his mother what he had done.

Isaiah 11:2
And the spirit of the LORD shall rest upon him, the spirit of wisdom and understanding, the spirit of counsel and might, the spirit of knowledge and of the fear of the LORD;

Proverbs 15:22
Without counsel purposes are disappointed: but in the multitude of counselors they are established."

Prayer
Father God I ask for a teachable and humble spirit that I may always seek wisdom and godly counsel for all matters. Holy Spirit please lead and guide me into all truth. I surrender my plans and agendas before you.

Proverbs 19:20-21
Hear counsel, and receive instruction, that thou mayest be wise in thy latter end. There are many devices in a man's heart; nevertheless the counsel of the Lord, that shall stand."

James 5:16
Confess your faults one to another, and pray one for another, that ye may be healed. The effectual fervent prayer of a righteous man availeth much.

Prayer
Father God, I ask for purity and transparency of heart to unveil matters of the heart. Please give me the spiritual maturity to bear someone's truth that healing may occur in the name of Jesus Christ

Angelic Assistance

Bless the Lord, ye his angels, that excel in strength, that do his commandments, hearkening unto the voice of his word.
Psalms 103:20

There are many events throughout scripture in which angels were used to communicate the will of God. Whether it was through dreams, vision or tangible manifestation angels were reverenced and their words were taken at face value.

Father God we welcome angelic intervention

Prayer Divine Assistance

Father God in heaven we look to the hills from whence comes our help and we ask for angelic assistance and intervention. Which You have made available to us by your own power and might. Lord you have given your angels charge over the righteous to keep us and protect us. May Your angels who excel in strength to do your will lead and guide us into the purpose you have predestined for our lives.

Lord God I ask You to utter your voice today against every spiritual army and force, great is your army. Let the elite in your army destroy the weapons of demonic princes, powers and rulers of darkness.

Let every demonic power standing against myself, my family, church and ministry this day receive the relentless fury of archangel Michael in the name of Jesus Christ. We receive from you Father God, the necessary help, angelic visitation, revelation, dreams and visions that will assist in propelling and advancing Your holy kingdom. Thank you for the instruction and direction we are in your service...

Joel 2:11
The Lord gives voice before His army, For His camp is very great; for strong is the One who executes His word: for the day of the Lord is great and very terrible; and who can abide it?

Exodus 33:2
And I will send an angel before thee; and I will drive out the Canaanite, the Amorite, and the Hittite, and the Perizzite, the Hivite, and the Jebusite:

Matthew 4:11
Then the devil leaveth him, and, behold, angels came and ministered unto him

Psalms 35:5-6
Let them be as chaff before the wind: and let the angel of the LORD chase *them*. Let their way be dark and slippery: and let the angel of the LORD persecute them.

Psalms 68:17
The chariots of God *are* twenty thousand, *even* thousands of angels: the Lord *is* among them, *as in* Sinai, in the holy *place*.

Isaiah 37:36
Then the angel of the LORD went forth, and smote in the camp of the Assyrians a hundred and fourscore and five thousand: and when they arose early in the morning, behold, they *were* all dead corpses.

Psalms 91:11
For he shall give his angels charge over thee, to keep thee in all thy ways.

Psalms 103:20

Bless the LORD, ye his angels, that excel in strength, that do his commandments, hearkening unto the voice of his word.

Psalms 34:7

The angel of the LORD encampeth round about them that fear him, and delivereth them.

Exodus 23:20-23

Behold, I send an Angel before thee, to keep thee in the way, and to bring thee into the place which I have prepared.

Prayer

Father God I thank you for sending angels to keep me and bringing me to the prepared place.

Numbers 20:16

And when we cried unto the LORD, he heard our voice, and sent an angel, and hath brought us forth out of Egypt: and, behold, we *are* in Kadesh, a city in the uttermost of thy border:

Animalistic Spirits

And God said, Let us make man in our image, after our likeness: and let them have dominion over the fish of the sea, and over the fowl of the air, and over the cattle, and over all the earth, and over every creeping thing that creepth upon the earth.
Genesis 1:26

All flesh is not the same flesh: but there is one kind of flesh of men, another flesh of beast, another of fishes, and another of birds.
1 Corinthians 15:39

We see in the book of Genesis that God created all things including animals. In chapter 3 of Genesis we learn that the serpent was more subtil than any of the beast created; he spoke with Eve which led to Eve eating fruit from the tree.

One conversation with the serpent caused tremendous consequences for all mankind. It is important to make sure we not only know who we are communicating with. But the source behind the conversation. Who are you communicating with?

What can we take away from the story of Eve and the serpent? But I would like to focus on animals like the serpent. There are many animals throughout scripture that are used for symbolism of their behavior or nature, many animals have certain attributes that are well known for example: cows give milk, bears devour and she bears protect their young, hyenas giggle, laugh and mock, eagles have great eyesight and are swift in flight, just to name a few.

Here we see in Matthew 25:32-33 the comparison between sheep and goats. *And before him shall be gathered all nations: and he shall separate them one from another, as a shepherd divideth his sheep from the goats: And he shall set the sheep on his right hand, but the goats on the left.*

We can see a greater example in Genesis 41 as Joseph interprets the Pharaoh dream regarding the kine also known as cow. What we can come to understand is that these positive and negative attributes of animals are used often in scripture and in the realm of the spirit.

In Prayer Artillery Volume 2 The Prophetic Office of A Dreamer we will learn more about animal symbolism as it relates to dreams and visions. No matter what the nature of the demonic animal we have certainly been given dominion over all according to Genesis 1:26-31.

With that being said I would like to take a look at the animals in which God classified as abominable. Understanding what God thinks concerning the nature of certain animals will bring clarity to the prayers contained in this book relating to animals. Let's look at these scriptures to see what is abominable.

Abominable Animals
Leviticus 11:4-8
Nevertheless, among those that chew the cud or part the hoof, you shall not eat these: The camel, because it chews the cud but does not part the hoof, is unclean to you.

And the rock badger, because it chews the cud but does not part the hoof, is unclean to you. And the hare, because it chews the cud but does not part the hoof, is unclean to you. And the pig, because it parts the hoof and is cloven-footed but does not chew the cud, is unclean to you. You shall not eat any of their flesh, and you shall not touch their carcasses; they are unclean to you.

Leviticus 11:10-20
But anything in the seas or the rivers that does not have fins and scales, of the swarming creatures in the waters and of the living creatures that are in the waters, is detestable to you. You shall regard them as detestable; you shall not eat any of their flesh, and you shall detest their carcasses. Everything in the waters that does not have fins and scales is detestable to you.

And these you shall detest among the birds; they shall not be eaten; they are detestable: the eagle, the bearded vulture, the black vulture, the kite, the falcon of any kind, every raven of any kind, he ostrich, the nighthawk, the seagull, the hawk of any kind, the little owl, the cormorant, the short-eared owl, the barn owl, the tawny owl, the carrion vulture, the stork, the heron of any kind, the hoopoe, and the bat. "All winged insects that go on all fours are detestable to you.

Now that we have an idea of the abominable animals let's look at animals in scripture that are depicted for their nature and qualities.

Bears
2 Kings 2:24
And he turned back, and looked on them, and cursed them in the name of the LORD. And there came forth two she bears out of the wood, and tare forty and two children of them.

Goats
Matthew 25:32-33
And before him shall be gathered all nations: and he shall separate them one from another, as a shepherd divideth *his* sheep from the goats: And he shall set the sheep on his right hand, but the goats on the left.

Wolves (Deception)
Matthew 7:15
Beware of false prophets, which come to you in sheep's clothing, but inwardly they are ravening wolves.

<u>**Lions**</u> (Devourer)
1 Peter 5:8
Be sober, be vigilant; because your adversary the devil, as a roaring lion, walketh about, seeking whom he may devour:

Psalms 10:9
He lieth in wait secretly as a lion in his den: he lieth in wait to catch the poor: he doth catch the poor, when he draweth him into his net.

When faced with spirit beings with the attributes of the animals mentioned above we must take authority through prayer with the aid of the Lord Jesus Christ. The bible tells us in 1 Peter 5:8 that our enemy and adversary, which is the devil, seeks to devour us. He walks around as a roaring lion. He seeks only to devour so we must remain sober and vigilant against his attempts for our lives through prayer.

LIONS, TIGERS AND BEARS OH MY!

As we follow the righteous path, the way of the Lord or what I call the yellow brick road with prayer to the glorious victory that has been established through Jesus Christ. We will flourish triumphantly... So again I say follow, follow the yellow brick road. Where victory has already been mapped out through Jesus Christ.

Prayer
I rebuke in the name of Jesus lurking lions, Father in the name of Jesus expose lions that are waiting secretly.

Judges 14:5-6
Then went Samson down, and his father and his mother, to Timnath, and came to the vineyards of Timnath: and, behold, a young lion roared against him. And the Spirit of the LORD came mightily upon him, and he rent him as he would have rent a kid, and he had nothing in his hand: but he told not his father or his mother what he had done.

Prayer Against Demonic Animals
Let every demonic lion on the hunt starve of hunger in Jesus name. Father God through your strength may the jaw of lions be broken and crushed. Remove from the lion's mouth the spoils captured. May every demonic lion hear the greater roar of Jesus Christ and flee.

Psalms 91:3
I tread upon lions in Jesus Name.

Psalms 57:4
My Soul is delivered from the snare of men who are like lions seeking to devour.

Leopards (God's Judgment)

Jeremiah 5:6

Wherefore a lion out of the forest shall slay them, *and* a wolf of the evenings shall spoil them, a leopard shall watch over their cities: every one that goeth out thence shall be torn in pieces: because their transgressions are many, *and* their backslidings are increased

Birds
Psalms 8:8

The fowl of the air, and the fish of the sea, and whatsoever passeth through the paths of the seas.

Prayer Against Demonic Fowl

I take dominion over the unclean fowl of the air in the name of Jesus Christ. Every spirit bird sent to monitor the affairs of my family, my life, ministry and church be bound in Jesus Christ name. May your silver cord be severed forever and burned by holy fire in Jesus Christ name.

Matthew 13:4

and as he sowed, some seeds fell beside the road, and the birds came and ate them up

Jeremiah 5:27

As a cage is full of birds, so *are* their houses full of deceit: therefore they are become great, and waxen rich.

Prayer

I bind and destroy and permanently cage every spiritual vulture, Lilith, owl, pelican, bittern, raven, hawk and demonic eagles. Be caged now in Jesus Christ name!

Job 28:7, 21

here is a path which no fowl knoweth, and which the vulture's eye hath not seen: Seeing it is hid from the eyes of all living, and kept close from the fowls of the air.

Prayer

I pray for the grace and wisdom to walk in paths unknown and hidden from demonic fowls in Jesus Christ might name.

I bind any unclean bird from nesting in my life, home, marriage and ministry. May every bird's nest be destroyed by fire in Jesus name.

<u>Vultures</u>
Revelation 18:2

Babylon the Great is described as being "a dwelling place of demons, a prison for every foul spirit, and a cage for every unclean and hated bird."

Genesis 15:11

And when the vultures came down on the carcasses, Abram drove them away.

Snakes
Genesis 3:1
Now the serpent was more subtil than any beast of the field which the Lord God had made. And he said unto the woman, Yea, hath God said, Ye shall not eat of every tree of the garden?

Jeremiah 8:17
Now the serpent was more subtil than any beast of the field which the Lord God had made. And he said unto the woman, Yea, hath God said, Ye shall not eat of every tree of the garden?

Matthew 10:16
Behold, I send you forth as sheep in the midst of wolves: be ye therefore wise as serpents, and harmless as doves.

Matthew 23:33
Ye serpents, ye generation of vipers, how can ye escape the damnation of hell?

Prayers Against Vipers/Snakes
Father in the name of Jesus spoil the fruit of python and the cohorts of religious spirits, pride, destruction, divination, familiar spirits and necromancer. I call each to never return again in the name of Jesus Christ. Let every serpent's head be bruised by the soles of my feet in the name of Jesus Christ.

Lord Jesus I ask that you will judge every disobedient and stubborn spirit against my life.

Psalm 91:3
For it is He who delivers you from the snare of the trapper
And from the deadly pestilence.

2 Corinthians 11:3
But I fear, lest by any means, as the serpent beguiled Eve through his subtilty, so your minds should be corrupted from the simplicity that is in Christ.

Prayer
I bind and rebuke the snake's scheme and plan of deception against my life.
Father God bind the spirit of python, that comes to squeeze financial blessings and life strength in Jesus Christ name.

I bind every venomous attack of the king cobra and the cockatrice now. In Jesus Christ mighty name!

Luke 10:19
Behold, I give unto you power to tread on serpents and scorpions, and over all the power of the enemy: and nothing shall by any means hurt you.

Prayer

I exercise my power, authority and dominion to tread over serpents and scorpions and over all the power of the enemy and the kingdom of darkness. And according to your word nothing shall hurt me.

Dragon
Revelation 12:9
And the great dragon was thrown down, the serpent of old who is called the devil and Satan, who deceives the whole world; he was thrown down to the earth, and his angels were thrown down with him

Isaiah 27:1
In that day the LORD with his sore and great and strong sword shall punish leviathan the piercing serpent, even leviathan that crooked serpent; and he shall slay the dragon that *is* in the sea.

Alligator / Crocodile / Leviathan
Job 41:1-34
Canst thou draw out leviathan with an hook? or his tongue with a cord which thou lettest down?

Canst thou put an hook into his nose? or bore his jaw through with a thorn?

Will he make many supplications unto thee? will he speak soft words unto thee?

Will he make a covenant with thee? wilt thou take him for a servant for ever?

Wilt thou play with him as with a bird? or wilt thou bind him for thy maidens?

Shall the companions make a banquet of him? shall they part him among the merchants?

Canst thou fill his skin with barbed irons? or his head with fish spears?

Lay thine hand upon him, remember the battle, do no more.

Behold, the hope of him is in vain: shall not one be cast down even at the sight of him?

None is so fierce that dare stir him up: who then is able to stand before me?

Who hath prevented me, that I should repay him? whatsoever is under the whole heaven is mine.

I will not conceal his parts, nor his power, nor his comely proportion.

Who can discover the face of his garment? or who can come to him with his double bridle?

Who can open the doors of his face? his teeth are terrible round about.

His scales are his pride, shut up together as with a close seal.

One is so near to another, that no air can come between them.

They are joined one to another, they stick together, that they cannot be sundered.

By his neesings a light doth shine, and his eyes are like the eyelids of the morning.

Out of his mouth go burning lamps, and sparks of fire leap out.

Out of his nostrils goeth smoke, as out of a seething pot or caldron.

His breath kindleth coals, and a flame goeth out of his mouth.

In his neck remaineth strength, and sorrow is turned into joy before him.

The flakes of his flesh are joined together: they are firm in themselves; they cannot be moved.

His heart is as firm as a stone; yea, as hard as a piece of the nether millstone.

When he raiseth up himself, the mighty are afraid: by reason of breakings they purify themselves.

The sword of him that layeth at him cannot hold: the spear, the dart, nor the habergeon.

He esteemeth iron as straw, and brass as rotten wood.

The arrow cannot make him flee: slingstones are turned with him into stubble.

Darts are counted as stubble: he laugheth at the shaking of a spear.

Sharp stones are under him: he spreadeth sharp pointed things upon the mire.

He maketh the deep to boil like a pot: he maketh the sea like a pot of ointment.

He maketh a path to shine after him; one would think the deep to be hoary.

Upon earth there is not his like, who is made without fear.

He beholdeth all high things: he is a king over all the children of pride.

Bats / Vampires
Proverbs 30:14
There is a generation, whose teeth *are as* swords, and their jaw teeth *as* knives, to devour the poor from off the earth, and the needy from among men.

Mouse
Isaiah 66:17
"Those who sanctify and purify themselves to go to the gardens, following one in the center, who eat swines flesh, detestable things and mice, will come to an end altogether," declares the Lord.

Leviticus 11:29
Now these are to you the unclean among the swarming things which swarm on the earth: the mole, and the mouse, and the great lizard in its kinds

Eagle

Lamentations 4:19
Our persecutors are swifter than the eagles of the heaven: they pursued us upon the mountains, they laid wait for us in the wilderness.

Revelation 12:14
And to the woman were given two wings of a great eagle, that she might fly into the wilderness, into her place, where she is nourished for a time, and times, and half a time, from the face of the serpent.

Exodus 19:4
Ye have seen what I did unto the Egyptians, and how I bare you on eagles' wings, and brought you unto myself.

Proverbs 30:19
he way of an eagle in the sky, the way of a serpent on a rock the way of a ship on the high seas, and the way of a man with a virgin

Jeremiah 48:40-44
For thus saith the LORD; Behold, he shall fly as an eagle, and shall spread his wings over Moab.
Kerioth is taken, and the strongholds are surprised, and the mighty men's hearts in Moab at that day shall be as the heart of a woman in her pangs.

And Moab shall be destroyed from *being* a people, because he hath magnified *himself* against the LORD.

Fear, and the pit, and the snare, *shall be* upon thee, O inhabitant of Moab, saith the LORD.

He that fleeth from the fear shall fall into the pit; and he that getteth up out of the pit shall be taken in the snare: for I will bring upon it, *even* upon Moab, the year of their visitation, saith the LORD.

Isaiah 40:31
but they who wait for the LORD shall renew their strength; they shall mount up with wings like eagles; they shall run and not be weary; they shall walk and not faint.

Psalms 103:5
who satisfies you with good so that your youth is renewed like the eagle's.

Jeremiah 49:22
Behold, he shall come up and fly as the eagle, and spread his wings over Bozrah: and at that day shall the heart of the mighty men of Edom be as the heart of a woman in her pangs.

Obadiah 1:4
Though thou exalt *thyself* as the eagle, and though thou set thy nest among the stars, thence will I bring thee down, saith the LORD.

Chapter 2
Charismatic Witchcraft
Prayer Artillery
Higher Levels of Prayer
For
End Time Strategic Warfare

For rebellion is as the sin of witchcraft, and stubbornness is as iniquity and idolatry. Because thou hast rejected the word of the Lord*, he hath also rejected thee from being king.*
1 Samuel 15:23

There are times in which we seek answers and direction from God. However, the response from God may not come when we would like. There are cases in the bible in which God was sought and He did not answer the prayer or request by dreams, visions, Urims and prophets.

In 1 Samuel 28 we see that king Saul was seeking direction from God. Because of his rebellion Saul did not receive a response. So Saul turned to the witch of Endor for answers.

We must remain in obedience with the Lord and keep His righteousness first in our lives. If we are seeking the presence of God, deliverance, answers, gifts from God, direction from God and promotion from God we must wait on Him.

Prayer is relational with God we must not become as Saul and many others throughout scripture seeking other vices and spiritual counsel through ungodly methods. We must remain in our lane which is a path of righteousness.

Prayer Against Divination

Father in heaven let the banner of righteous overshadow me this day. According to Matthew 6:33 I will seek first Your holy kingdom and things that pertain to Your righteous rule.

I reject and denounce a spirit of self rule and self righteousness. The steps of a good man are ordered by You my Lord. As I walk righteously You will have delight in me. And though I may fail You will not cast me down, Lord you will uphold me according to Psalms 37:23-24. *The steps of a good man are ordered by the LORD: and he delighteth in his way. Though he fall, he shall not be utterly cast down: for the LORD upholdeth him with his hand.*

What did king Saul do?

As we read the verses below, we will discover what king Saul did, why he did it and what his consequence was.

1 Samuel 28:6-10

And when Saul enquired of the LORD, the LORD answered him not, neither by dreams, nor by Urim, nor by prophets. Then said Saul unto his servants, Seek me a woman that hath a familiar spirit, that I may go to her, and enquire of her.

And his servants said to him, Behold, there is a woman that hath a familiar spirit at Endor.

And Saul disguised himself, and put on other raiment, and he went, and two men with him, and they came to the woman by night: and he said, I pray thee, divine unto me by the familiar spirit, and bring me him up, whom I shall name unto thee.

And the woman said unto him, Behold, thou knowest what Saul hath done, how he hath cut off those that have familiar spirits, and the wizards, out of the land: wherefore then layest thou a snare for my life, to cause me to die? And Saul sware to her by the LORD, saying, As the LORD liveth, there shall no punishment happen to thee for this thing.

> *So Saul died for his transgression which he committed against the LORD, even against the word of the LORD, which he kept not, and also for asking counsel of one that had a familiar spirit, to enquire of it;*
>
> *And enquired not of the LORD: therefore he slew him, and turned the kingdom unto David the son of Jesse.*
>
> *1 Chronicles 10:13-14*

What did Manasseh do?

There are some common attributes between king Saul and Manasseh. In 2 Chronicles 33 we will also see what Manasseh did, why he did it and what consequence he faced.

2 Chronicles 33:6

Manasseh was twelve years old when he began to reign, and he reigned fifty and five years in Jerusalem: But did that which was evil in the sight of the LORD, like unto the abominations of the heathen, whom the LORD had cast out before the children of Israel. For he built again the high places which Hezekiah his father had broken down, and he reared up altars for Baalim, and made groves, and worshiped all the host of heaven, and served them.

Also he built altars in the house of the LORD, whereof the LORD had said, In Jerusalem shall my name be for ever. And he built altars for all the host of heaven in the two courts of the house of the LORD. And he caused his children to pass through the fire in the valley of the son of Hinnom: also he observed times, and used enchantments, and used witchcraft, and dealt with a familiar spirit, and with wizards: he wrought much evil in the sight of the LORD, to provoke him to anger.

And the LORD spake to Manasseh, and to his people: but they would not hearken. Wherefore the LORD brought upon them the captains of the host of the king of Assyria, which took Manasseh among the thorns, and bound him with fetters, and carried him to Babylon.

And when he was in affliction, he besought the LORD his God, and humbled himself greatly before the God

of his fathers, And prayed unto him: and he was
intreated of him, and heard his supplication, and
brought him again to Jerusalem into his kingdom.
Then Manasseh knew that the LORD he was God.
2 Chronicles 33:10-13

Again, there is a common thread between king Saul and king
Manasseh; the most obvious is that they were both kings who
allowed pride and disobedience to guide them. They rebelled
against God, and like Humpty Dumpty they had a great fall.

And all the kings men could not put Humpty Dumpty back
together again. Proverbs 16:18-20 *Pride goeth before*
destruction, and an haughty spirit before a fall. Better it is to
be of an humble spirit with the lowly, than to divide the spoil
with the proud. He that handleth a matter wisely shall find
good: and whoso trusteth in the LORD, happy is he.

They expected God to receive them and keep the lines of
support, communication and blessing open even when they
were disobedient and rebellious. From these two stories of
Saul and Manasseh in the scripture is this how God almighty
operates?

What is the difference according to the scriptures referenced
between king Saul and king Manasseh? We find that King
Manasseh humbled himself and prayed to God when he was
afflicted. And God heard ... We must always be mindful to
humble ourselves before God.

Prayer of Humility

Father God, we ask that You would keep us God centered. Place within me the right hearts necessary for pleasing You. I ask you of the Holy Spirit to be my daily guide and truth compass. I pray to remain humble and display meekness. May I always seek You for counsel and direction. In Jesus Christ name ... Thank you!

Revelation 22:15

For without are dogs, and sorcerers, and whoremongers, and murderers, and idolaters, and whosoever loveth and maketh a lie.

Leviticus 19:31

Regard not them that have familiar spirits, neither seek after wizards, to be defiled by them: I am the Lord your God.

Leviticus 20:27

A man also or woman that hath a familiar spirit, or that is a wizard, shall surely be put to death: they shall stone them with stones: their blood shall be upon them.

Galatians 5:17-21

For the flesh lusteth against the Spirit, and the Spirit against the flesh: and these are contrary the one to the other: so that ye cannot do the things that ye would. But if ye be led of the Spirit, ye are not under the law. Now the works of the flesh are manifest, which are these;

Adultery, fornication, uncleanness, lasciviousness, Idolatry, witchcraft, hatred, variance, emulations, wrath, strife, seditions, heresies, Envyings, murders, drunkenness, revellings, and such like: of the which I tell you before, as I have also told you in time past, that they which do such things shall not inherit the kingdom of God.

We must repent for any of these activities
Once repented we can now bind them...

If I regard iniquity in my heart, the Lord will not hear me: But verily God hath heard me; he hath attended to the voice of my prayer. Blessed be God, which hath not turned away my prayer, nor his mercy from me. Psalms 66:18-20

Prayer

Father in the matchless name of Jesus Christ I ask that you destroy all foundational demonic powers in operation in my life, my family, my church, my city and my nation(s).

I bind and break all powers of :
Denominational spirits of control/manipulation and dictatorial Erroneous belief
Discord
Demonic betrayal of charismatic manifestation
Ruling demons over pastors and leaders of church organizations
Jezel, Ahab

Passivity/Mind control and confusion
Rejection by christians
False worship, false teachers, false apostles, false prophets
Demonic tongues
False grace/False humility
Charismatic witchcraft, occult dealings, warlocks
Ungodly intercession and prayers
False prophecies
Mammon message, greed and covetousness
Divination
Favoritism and nepotism
Spiritual pride/Idolatry
False visions and false dreams
Worship of Men and fear of men
Catholicism, masonry, mormonism, antichrist religions
Spiritual fantasies and false love
Ancestral worship
Idolizing the dead, former relatives etc.
In Jesus Christ name...Amen!

Defeating Giants

When we are faced with giants, meaning situations, circumstances, people, places and things we must be ready to fight against all the enemies that defy the Lord God. Remember David had five stones but it only took one stone to the forehead to lay out Goliath and sword to cut his head off.

Then said David to the Philistine, Thou comest to me with a sword, and with a spear, and with a shield: but I come to thee in the name of the LORD of hosts, the God of the armies of Israel, whom thou hast defied.

Prayer Against Spiritual Giants

I will fight the good fight of faith in the name of Jesus Christ. I place upon myself the armor of the Lord God. I stand in these evil days with my entire being consumed with the truth of the word of God. And with the shield of faith I block every demonic dart targeted against my life.

I command every dart fired against me to be returned to the pit of hell in the name of Jesus Christ. I command every spiritual Goliath to die now in the name of Jesus Christ. I release upon every giant the five smooth stones of prayer, the name of the Lord, obedience to God's word, faith in God and a servant's heart in the name of Jesus Christ.

Which stone will you aim at the forehead of your giant(s)?

1 Samuel 17:49

And David put his hand in his bag, and took thence a stone, and slang *it*, and smote the Philistine in his forehead, that the stone sunk into his forehead; and he fell upon his face to the earth

Chapter 3
Dismantling Demonic Confederacies
Prayer Artillery
Higher Levels of Prayer
For
End Time Strategic Warfare

O God the Lord, the strength of my salvation, thou hast covered my head in the day of battle.   Psalms 140:7

A confederacy according to the Oxford Dictionary is: *an alliance of people or groups formed for an illicit purpose.* Illicit by definition is: *forbidden by law, rules, or custom.*

Which brings us to the understanding that demonic confederations are those which have come into alliance to steal, kill and destroy. We must take a bold stand for the Kingdom of God and rebuke and bind all of that which is illicit, illegal, unlawful, outlawed and against the righteousness of God.

As we begin to dismantle coalitions, confederations, leagues of demons and associations through the word of God by prayer, heaven will fight with us for the righteousness of our homes, families, churchs, cities and governments.

However, we must oil our elbows and knees and put in the work. 1 Corinthians 3:9 *For we are labourers together with*

God: ye are God's husbandry, ye are God's building. Before we can effectively build the strong man must be subdued.

Prayer Against Spiritual Confederations
Father God in heaven, bind all kings, princes, rulers of darkness in high places, in the name of Jesus Christ let them be stripped bare of hierarchy, rank, armor and powers. Father God let each be separated from another and break the four witch covenant agreement.

Father in heaven disappoint the devices of the crafty, so that their hands cannot perform their enterprises Job 5:12. Father in heaven send your warring angels to bind the spirits responsible for these wicked actions, bind them in chains and muzzle and gag their speech till the day of judgment. In Jesus Christ might name.

Obadiah 1:7
All the men of thy confederacy have brought thee *even* to the border: the men that were at peace with thee have deceived thee, *and* prevailed against thee; *they that eat* thy bread have laid a wound under thee: *there is* none understanding in him.

Prayer
Let every demonic confederacy be scattered and divided, let their ranks be put asunder and never rejoined. I raise a mighty sound of praise and worship to you Lord Jesus Christ that will bring confusion and chaos into their ranks that they may devour one another.

2 Chronicles 20:21-22 *And when he had consulted with the people, he appointed singers unto the L*ORD*, and that should praise the beauty of holiness, as they went out before the army, and to say, Praise the L*ORD*; for his mercy endureth for ever. And when they began to sing and to praise, the L*ORD *set ambushments against the children of Ammon, Moab, and mount Seir, which were come against Judah; and they were smitten.*

2 Chronicles 20:6 *And said, O L*ORD* God of our fathers, art not thou God in heaven? and rulest not thou over all the kingdoms of the heathen? and in thine hand is there not power and might, so that none is able to withstand thee?*

Prayer

Father in the name of Jesus Christ let confusion be released upon every demonic confederacy directed against my life, my family, my ministry, my church. Father in the name of Jesus Christ disperse all demonic reinforcements and retaliation squads in Jesus Christ name bring them to stubble before me Lord.

Psalms 149:1-9
*Praise ye the L*ORD*. Sing unto the L*ORD* a new song, and his praise in the congregation of saints.*

Let Israel rejoice in him that made him: let the children of Zion be joyful in their King.

Let them praise his name in the dance: let them sing praises unto him with the timbrel and harp.

For the LORD taketh pleasure in his people: he will beautify the meek with salvation.

Let the saints be joyful in glory: let them sing aloud upon their beds.

Let the high praises of God be in their mouth, and a two-edged sword in their hand;

To execute vengeance upon the heathen, and punishments upon the people;

To bind their kings with chains, and their nobles with fetters of iron;

To execute upon them the judgment written: this honor have all his saints. Praise ye the LORD.

Prayer

I war with the high praises of God in my mouth and a two edged sword in my hand that I may execute your vengeance upon every demonic confederacy. I release the judgment and punishment of Jehovah God to bind every demonic king in chains, and their demonic princes with fetters of iron. I execute upon these demonic confederate powers the judgment written in the name of Jesus Christ. Thank you Lord God for this is the honor you have given to us.

Psalms 83:13
O my God, make them like a wheel; as the stubble before the wind.

2 Chronicles 20:23
For the children of Ammon and Moab stood up against the inhabitants of mount Seir, utterly to slay and destroy *them*: and when they had made an end of the inhabitants of Seir, every one helped to destroy another. In the name of Jesus Christ let the ranks fall apart, let all those within the confederacy be turned to confuse and strike each other. Father in heaven let you battering ram annihilate every wall of evil confederacies let all barriers be broken in Jesus Christ name.

Hosea 10:2
Their heart is divided; now shall they be found faulty: he shall break down their altars, he shall spoil their images.

Destruction

Prayer Against Destruction
I shall not be afraid of the terror that storms the night. I bind the spirit of fear I walk in the liberty of perfect love. I am shielded with the breastplate of righteousness against all arrows from Satan in the mighty name of Jesus Christ. I bind all powers of witches and warlocks that walk in darkness. I ask Lord Jesus that their cloak and coverings be removed and let them be revealed.

Psalms 91:5-8

You shall not be afraid of the terror by night, Nor of the arrow that flies by day, Nor of the pestilence that walks in darkness, Nor of the destruction that lays waste at noonday. A thousand may fall at your side, And ten thousand at your right hand; But it shall not come near you. Only with your eyes shall you look, And see the reward of the wicked.

Prayer

I bind the spirit of terror and the spirit of fear, I break the power of your assignment in the mighty name of Jesus Christ. I reject all pride that goes before destruction. I will not succumb to a devilish appetite. I resist the urge for earthly things and vain desires in the name of Jesus Christ. According to Matthew 7:13 *Enter ye in at the strait gate: for wide is the gate, and broad is the way, that leadeth to destruction, and many there be which go in thereat:* I will enter through the narrow gate.

Philippians 3:18-19

(For many walk, of whom I have told you often, and now tell you even weeping, that they are the enemies of the cross of Christ:
Whose end is destruction, whose God is their belly, and whose glory is in their shame, who mind earthly things.)

1 Corinthians 5:5
Ye serpents, ye generation of vipers, how can ye escape the damnation of hell?

Proverbs 10:15
The rich man's wealth is his strong city: The destruction of the poor is their poverty. The labor of the righteous tendeth to life: The fruit of the wicked to sin.

The Devil

And the great dragon was cast out, that old serpent, called the Devil, and Satan, which deceiveth the whole world: he was cast out into the earth, and his angels were cast out with him
Revelation 12:9

We have learned through the scriptures that our battle is not against flesh and blood. However, humans can give themselves over as instruments of satanic use just as the believer gives over oneself for the service of the Lord Jesus Christ. However, we do have an adversary named Satan aka the devil who endeavors to destroy the saints of God. Pride runs through Satan's veins; he is seated in pride. God is love and Satan is pride...

Satan was ask this question, *how art thou fallen from heaven, O Lucifer, son of the morning! how art thou cut down to the ground, which didst weaken the nations! Isaiah 14:12*

For thou hast said in thine heart, I will ascend into heaven, I will exalt my throne above the stars of God: I will sit also upon the mount of the congregation, in the sides of the north: Isaiah 14:12-13

Satan answers why, *I will ascend above the heights of the clouds; I will be like the most High. Yet thou shalt be brought down to hell, to the sides of the pit. Isaiah 14:14*. Satan wanted to be God and take God's place in the heavens. There may be an innocence in wanting to emulate another person.

But when we seek to be the person and take their place we are operating satanically for positions, influence, people, places or things that God has not ascribed to our lives. This goes beyond covetousness; this is satanic; it is what Satan attempted to do with God the Father.

This is the move that led to the basis of the battle we face today between Satan and God in which Satan fell like lightning from the heavens. And he did not go alone; he took a third of the angels with him. So we must be vigilant and not take spiritual coups against our lives lightly.

Prayer Against Pride

May every satanic order and coup against my life be permanently paralyzed and dismantled by the blood of the Lord Jesus Christ. I bind the spirits of jealousy, pride, envy and covetousness against myself, my marriage, my family and ministry in Jesus Christ mighty name!

I resist religious pride, spiritual pride, terrestrial and celestial pride in the name of Jesus Christ! I bind to myself the way of humility and meekness. Glory to God forever!

So by all means reject and return pride to the sender when you find it operating in you or in your environment. To become effective in prayer and intercession we must resist spiritual pride; it is Jesus Christ that does the work in and through us. Demons are not subject to our name(s), but they are subject to the name of Jesus Christ. Praise the Living God forever!

Prayer

I release the name of Jesus, the name that is above all names. I release the name of Jesus into all areas of my life and the lives around. And I command every power and demon to respond and bow to the mighty name of Jesus Christ now! I command you Satan in the name of Jesus to pick up every weapon against my life and flee. I return every demonic vice to the sender in the name of Jesus Christ.
(Just take a moment here and began to call on the name of Jesus)

Philippians 2:10-11 *That at the name of Jesus every knee should bow, of things in heaven, and things in earth, and things under the earth; And that every tongue should confess that Jesus Christ is Lord, to the glory of God the Father.*

The only name Satan will respond to is Jesus Christ. Through the name of Jesus we have been given a badge of honor and authority to execute His will. With this badge of authority we have a right to bind, loose, chain, command, apprehend, arrest, tread upon, and subdue Satan and his cohorts in the name of Jesus Christ.

John 10:10-15
The thief cometh not, but for to steal, and to kill, and to destroy: I am come that they might have life, and that they might have it more abundantly. I am the good shepherd: the good shepherd giveth his life for the sheep.

But he that is a hireling, and not the shepherd, whose own the sheep are not, seeth the wolf coming, and leaveth the sheep, and fleeth: and the wolf catcheth them, and scattereth the sheep. The hireling fleeth, because he is an hireling, and careth not for the sheep. I am the good shepherd, and know my sheep, and am known of mine. As the Father knoweth me, even so know I the Father: and I lay down my life for the sheep.

Revelation 20:8-11
And shall go out to deceive the nations which are in the four quarters of the earth, Gog, and Magog, to gather them together to battle: the number of whom is as the sand of the sea. And they went up on the breadth of the earth, and compassed the camp of the saints about, and the beloved city:

and fire came down from God out of heaven, and devoured them.

And the devil that deceived them was cast into the lake of fire and brimstone, where the beast and the false prophet are, and shall be tormented day and night for ever and ever. And I saw a great white throne, and him that sat on it, from whose face the earth and the heaven fled away; and there was found no place for them.

Luke 10:16-20
He that heareth you heareth me; and he that despiseth you despiseth me; and he that despiseth me despiseth him that sent me.

And the seventy returned again with joy, saying, Lord, even the devils are subject unto us through thy name. And he said unto them, I beheld Satan as lightning fall from heaven.

Behold, I give unto you power to tread on serpents and scorpions, and over all the power of the enemy: and nothing shall by any means hurt you. Notwithstanding in this rejoice not, that the spirits are subject unto you; but rather rejoice, because your names are written in heaven.

Prayer

Satan the Lord rebuke you! You are a defeated foe Jesus Christ of Nazareth made a show of you openly on the cross. I decree I am vigilant against my adversary, the devil and his host.

I resist the workings of Satan in my life and I command you to flee in the name of Jesus according to James 4:7. *Submit yourselves therefore to God. Resist the devil, and he will flee from you.*

In Jesus Christ name I am released from every bondage of Satan and with the anointing of Jesus Christ let every yoke of bondage be destroyed and loosed according to Luke 13:16. *And ought not this woman, being a daughter of Abraham, whom Satan hath bound, lo, these eighteen years, be loosed from this bond on the sabbath day?*

I receive the supernatural grace of the Holy Spirit to prevail forward into success and prosperity. I command you Satan to get thee behind me in Jesus Name Luke 4:8.
And Jesus answered and said unto him, Get thee behind me, Satan: for it is written, Thou shalt worship the Lord thy God, and him only shalt thou serve.

Father in heaven nullify and blot out any and all ordinances written against my life. I receive the blood of Jesus Christ and the finished work of the cross by which I am made righteous.

Queen spirit

Prayer Against Queen and Goddess Spirits

I bind every demonic queen of Jezel, Athaliah, Delilah in Jesus Christ name. Father God bind every operation and strategy programmed by Astaroh, Issaichar, Semiramis, Diana, Isis, Venus and Artemis from deceptive operations. I stand as Jehu to slay every spirit of Jezebel in the name of Jesus Christ.

Judges 10:16

And they put away the strange gods from among them, and served the LORD: and his soul was grieved for the misery of Israel.

Prayer

I bind and rebuke every spirit of queendom that promotes witchcraft, perversion, religion, and diverse culture worship and rebellion in the name of Jesus Christ.

I bind all queens of catholicism, spirits of Fatima, Guadalupe, queen of saints and false worship to the queen of Mary go now in the name of Jesus Christ. Isaiah 47:5 *Sit thou silent, and get thee into darkness, O daughter of the Chaldeans: for thou shalt no more be called, The lady of kingdoms.*

I bind and rebuke the queen of the coast and of the seas from any covert and overt operation within my life or *(name)* in the mighty name of Jesus Christ.

Prayer

I bind and cast down every goddess operating in the lives of my family, ministry and church affiliation. I bind every demonic queen operating through the feminist movement. I bind every queen spirit responsible for sponsoring lesbianism. I cast down every spirit behind control and sexual manipulation.

I bind the spirit behind the seduction of clothing, cosmetics, false hair, false nails. I will not promote a demonic image through clothes, hair,

nails and makeup. I renounce all dealings and agreements with any items associated and offered as sacrifices and initiation to the kingdom of darkness.

Father in heaven I ask that you wash me from all unrighteousness and cleanse me in the power of the shed blood of Jesus Christ. Remove from me all spots and stains in the name of Jesus Christ.

Father in the name of Jesus remove me from any and all spiritual cages and uncover my soul from the pit and spirit from all darkness into the kingdom of light and let your glory be my defense.

Psalms 83:3-5

They have taken crafty counsel against thy people, and consulted against thy hidden ones. They have said, Come, and let us cut them off from being a nation; that the name of Israel may be no more in remembrance. For they have consulted together with one consent: they are confederate against thee:

Marine Spirits

Prayer Against Water and Marine Spirits

Father in the name of Jesus Christ let the rivers, the waters of the valley, the seas and the oceans be divided allow your righteous the way of passage to the promises and the land you have purposed. Father in the name of Jesus Christ cut the head off of every Leviathan, bind the workings of the octopus and the squid, let the waters of their habitation dry up.

Lord God, slay every dragon and hydra of the sea. Break the head of their power. Let a mighty spiritual drought destroy them. Let all spoils that have been held captive by the seas, the oceans, rivers, and valley springs be released in Jesus Christ might name Job 41:15. *His scales are his pride, shut up together as with a close seal.*

Let godly dreams, visions and creativity be restored in Jesus Christ's name. In the name of Jesus Christ I loose from myself pride, arrogance and haughtiness of spirit. I bind to myself the fruits of the

Holy Spirit according to Galatians 5:22-23.
But the fruit of the Spirit is *love, joy, peace, longsuffering, gentleness, goodness, faith, Meekness, temperance: against such there is no law.*

Psalms 18:40
Thou hast also given me the necks of mine enemies; that I might destroy them that hate me.

Luke 11:22
But when a stronger than he shall come upon him, and overcome him, he taketh from him all his armor wherein he trusted, and divideth his spoils.

Psalms 27:1
The LORD *is* my light and my salvation; whom shall I fear? the LORD *is* the strength of my life; of whom shall I be afraid?

Psalms 74:13
The LORD *is* my light and my salvation; whom shall I fear? the LORD *is* the strength of my life; of whom shall I be afraid? Thou brakest the heads of leviathan in pieces, *and* gavest him *to be* meat to the people inhabiting the wilderness. Thou didst cleave the fountain and the flood: thou driedst up mighty rivers.

Job 41:1-2

Canst thou draw out leviathan with an hook? or his tongue with a cord which thou lettest down? Canst thou put an hook into his nose? or bore his jaw through with a thorn?

Jeremiah 51:36

Therefore thus saith the LORD; Behold, I will plead thy cause, and take vengeance for thee; and I will dry up her sea, and make her springs dry.

Job 9:13

If God will not withdraw his anger, the proud helpers do stoop under him.

Isaiah 44:27

That confirmeth the word of his servant, and performeth the counsel of his messengers; that saith to Jerusalem, Thou shalt be inhabited; and to the cities of Judah, Ye shall be built, and I will raise up the decayed places thereof:

That saith to the deep, Be dry, and I will dry up thy rivers:

That saith of Cyrus, He is my shepherd, and shall perform all my pleasure: even saying to Jerusalem, Thou shalt be built; and to the temple, Thy foundation shall be laid.

Marriage

Holy matrimony is one of the greatest institutions established on earth between men and women. God has ordained marriage and called it holy. It was God who presented Eve to Adam. It was God who made Eve for Adam. We see this in Genesis 2:21-24 *"And the LORD God caused a deep sleep to fall upon Adam, and he slept: and he took*

one of his ribs, and closed up the flesh instead thereof; And the rib, which the LORD God had taken from man, made he a woman, and brought her unto the man. And Adam said, This is now bone of my bones, and flesh of my flesh: she shall be called Woman, because she was taken out of Man. Therefore shall a man leave his father and his mother, and shall cleave unto his wife: and they shall be one flesh."

My Prayer For You!

If you are and you desire a mate ...

Father God in heaven I pray for those who are seeking and believing You for a destiny mate. I ask that their marital glory appear and manifest. Father God if you are not behind the marital delay break and destroy the powers that are. I speak the blood of Jesus Christ against every root to maritals problems. Father God according to your word a help meet was made for Adam. I ask You to orchestrate a divine meeting and appointment with the women and men reading this prayer. Lord allow that woman to encounter her Adam and allow that man to encounter his Eve. I decree and declare marital breakthroughs in the mighty name of Jesus. I pray that you will be located for marital success!

Prayer For Godly Marriage

Father in heaven I thank you for holy matrimony You Lord God established the marriage covenant between man and women. May my marriage always be held in high honor according to your word. I will use my words as honey to pour over my wife/husband may my words bring comfort, strength and renewal.

May my character and nature toward my spouse be seasoned with wisdom, understanding and knowledge. Lord I bind to my marriage Ephesians 5:25-33

Husbands, love your wives, even as Christ also loved the church, and gave himself for it;

That he might sanctify and cleanse it with the washing of water by the word,

That he might present it to himself a glorious church, not having spot, or wrinkle, or any such thing; but that it should be holy and without blemish.

So ought men to love their wives as their own bodies. He that loveth his wife loveth himself.

For no man ever yet hated his own flesh; but nourisheth and cherisheth it, even as the Lord the church:

For we are members of his body, of his flesh, and of his bones.

For this cause shall a man leave his father and mother, and shall be joined unto his wife, and they two shall be one flesh.

This is a great mystery: but I speak concerning Christ and the church.

Nevertheless let every one of you in particular so love his wife even as himself; and the wife see that she reverence her husband.

The Ephesians Prayer

Ephesians 5:25-33
Husbands, love your wives, even as Christ also loved the church, and gave himself for it;
(I will love my mate I will be selfless and giving)

That he might sanctify and cleanse it with the washing of water by the word,
(We will allow the word of the God to cleanse our ways and motives in our marriage)

That he might present it to himself a glorious church, not having spot, or wrinkle, or any such thing; but that it should be holy and without blemish.
(The prayer is to present a glorious marriage that is in alignment with the will of our heavenly Father God)

So ought men to love their wives as their own bodies. He that loveth his wife loveth himself.
(We will not abuse one another with words, we will not take one another for granted we decree and declare that our marriage is founded in the principles of love and thanksgiving)

For no man ever yet hated his own flesh; but nourisheth and cherisheth it, even as the Lord the church:
(We will cherish one another to the glory of God, offering praise and thanks for the opportunity to share a good godly life)

For we are members of his body, of his flesh, and of his bones.
(We are part of the body of Jesus Christ and present our time, gifts and talents to the service of Jehovah God. We reject competing with our own flesh for we are one)

For this cause shall a man leave his father and mother, and shall be joined unto his wife, and they two shall be one flesh.
(For this cause God our Father has joined us together, we are one, we disallow disagreements, strife, contentions, people, places and things to separate the love of God in our marriage for this is the great covenant of God in the name of Jesus Christ)

This is a great mystery: but I speak concerning Christ and the church. Nevertheless let every one of you in particular so love his wife even as himself; and the wife see that she reverence her husband

Genesis 24:40
And he said unto me, The LORD, before whom I walk, will send his angel with thee, and prosper thy way; and thou shalt take a wife for my son of my kindred, and of my father's house:

Marital Delay

Psalms 31:14-15
My times *are* in thy hand: deliver me from the hand of mine enemies, and from them that persecute me.

Psalms 20:4
Grant thee according to thine own heart, and fulfill all thy counsel.

Isaiah 34:16
Seek ye out of the book of the LORD, and read: no one of these shall fail, none shall want her mate: for my mouth it hath commanded, and his spirit it hath gathered them.

Prayer Against Marital Delay
With the power and authority given to me through Jesus Christ I bind ancestral bondage, evil altars and spiritual cages promoting marital delay. In Jesus name I die by the fire of God now!

I loose myself in the mighty name of Jesus Christ from evil covenants, local wickedness, household witchcraft, decrees, curses and witchcraft powers.

I bind to myself the blood of Jesus Christ. I receive full victory against every spirit of delay. I decree that your tenure is over in the mighty name of Jesus Christ.

Father God in heaven let all spirit husbands and wives be permanently bound and chained. Let every demonic marital covenant with any spirit husband and wife be destroyed by the blood of Jesus Christ. Let every evil mark of rejection and loneliness be permanently washed and removed from my face in the name of Jesus Christ.

I bind the spirit of Deliah, spirit of the mermaid, queen of the coast, Jezebel and all marine witchcraft attacking and withholding my marriage to go now in Jesus Christ name. Lord Jesus Christ I ask that you would baptize me with the Holy Spirit and with fire.

I rebuke and bind all spiritual blindness fired against my marital destiny in the name of Jesus Christ. My marital mate will see me. I will not be overlooked, I bind all strange women and men releasing ungodly intercession and evil prayers against my wedding day in Jesus Christ name.

Decree and declare that my marital glory shall appear and manifest in my life. My God given and ordained spouse come forth now in Jesus Christ name. I receive the fragrance of the Lord Jesus Christ. I now walk in divine aroma. Glory to God forever!

Adultery

The greatest covenant is between husband and wife. The fellowship between a man and a woman is what Satan fears the most. We learn in Matthew 18:19 (*Again I say unto you, That if two of you shall agree on earth as touching anything that they shall ask, it shall be done for them of my Father which is in heaven.*) Satan fears this type of godly agreement because it comes with a promise that if two shall agree that it shall be done by God. If he can block and destroy godly marriages he can hinder the conception and birth of godly enterprise and purpose from coming forth on the earth.

We must fight on our knees for the sanctity of godly marriages with prayer. Praying as a couple is most important. When couples pray together it reinforces the agreement of God. And prayer propels the destiny of the marriage. Prayer also provides a protective shield against the enemy and the kingdom of darkness. If spouses don't pray one for the other their marriage could end up as prey for the enemy. I would like to offer seven points of wisdom for marriage:

1. Pray
2. Forgive
3. Pray Some More!
4. Forgive Some More!
5. Love
6. Hug
7. Kiss

You'd be surprised and amazed at how quickly a simple yet effective hug from a spouse could cast out a devil. *Laugh Out Loud* I pray that your marriage would be sweeter than honey, in fact that it would be so sugar sweet that it will give the enemy a toothache.

And we all know that you can get pregnant from kissing *Laugh out Loud*

Prayer Against Adultery

My marriage shall not fail, my marriage shall prevail no man or woman shall put asunder what the living God Jehovah has put together in the name Jesus Christ. I command every woman and man sent by the enemy to dissolve my marriage be apprehended and return to their sender with unfulfilled assignments in the name of Jesus!

Lord Jesus I ask that you will heal every broken heart and give healing balm to all areas of our lives that would serve as entry points for Satan to institute divisions. I decree and declare that I am free from all past mistakes, downfalls, relationships, people, places and things. I moreover declare that I am an instrument of love, peace and joy!

I am living the abundant Life in Christ Jesus

#TheMarriedLife

Proverbs 30:20

Such *is* the way of an adulterous woman; she eateth, and wipeth her mouth, and saith, I have done no wickedness.

Prayer

In the name of Jesus Christ we will flee fornication and perversion. Lord help us to walk in righteousness. We reject being joined to harlots and whoremongers. But Lord we are joined to you and the three of us are one flesh and one spirit.

1 Corinthians 6:15-20

Know ye not that your bodies are the members of Christ? shall I then take the members of Christ, and make them the members of an harlot? God forbid. What? know ye not that he which is joined to an harlot is one body? for two, saith he, shall be one flesh. But he that is joined unto the Lord is one spirit.

Flee fornication. Every sin that a man doeth is without the body; but he that committeth fornication sinneth against his own body. What? know ye not that your body is the temple of the Holy Ghost which is in you, which ye have of God, and ye are not your own? For ye are bought with a price: therefore glorify God in your body, and in your spirit, which are God's.

Proverbs 5:3-22
For the lips of a strange woman drop as an honeycomb, and
her mouth is smoother than oil: But her end is bitter as
wormwood, sharp as a two-edged sword. Her feet go down to
death; her steps take hold on hell. Lest thou shouldest ponder
the path of life, her ways are moveable, that thou canst not
know them. Hear me now therefore, O ye children, and
depart not from the words of my mouth.

Remove thy way far from her, and come not nigh the door of
her house: Lest thou give thine honor unto others, and thy
years unto the cruel: Lest strangers be filled with thy wealth;
and thy labors be in the house of a stranger;

And thou mourn at the last, when thy flesh and thy body are
consumed, And say, How have I hated instruction, and my
heart despised reproof;

And have not obeyed the voice of my teachers, nor inclined
mine ear to them that instructed me! I was almost in all evil in
the midst of the congregation and assembly. Drink waters out
of thine own cistern, and running waters out of thine own
well.

Let thy fountains be dispersed abroad, and rivers of waters in
the streets. Let them be only thine own, and not strangers'
with thee. Let thy fountain be blessed: and rejoice with the
wife of thy youth. Let her be as the loving hind and pleasant

roe; let her breasts satisfy thee at all times; and be thou ravished always with her love.

And why wilt thou, my son, be ravished with a strange woman, and embrace the bosom of a stranger? For the ways of man are before the eyes of the LORD, and he pondereth all his goings. His own iniquities shall take the wicked himself, and he shall be holden with the cords of his sins.

Mark 10:9
What therefore God hath joined together, let not man put asunder.

Man for Woman Marriage

In the book of Genesis God created a woman for Adam and of course Adam was a man. With this creation of man and woman they were expected to be fruitful, multiply and replenish the earth. As a result of them being fruitful we are here; you and me. The holy bible does not make mention of male and male, nor female to female. Genesis 5:1-2
This is the book of the generations of Adam. In the day that God created man, in the likeness of God made he him; Male and female created he them; and blessed them, and called their name Adam, in the day when they were created.

God created the biology of man and woman to produce and multiply after its own kind. Below are some scriptures that reinforce the creation plan of God.

Romans 1:17-32

For therein is the righteousness of God revealed from faith to faith: as it is written, The just shall live by faith. For the wrath of God is revealed from heaven against all ungodliness and unrighteousness of men, who hold the truth in unrighteousness;

Because that which may be known of God is manifest in them; for God hath shewed it unto them. For the invisible things of him from the creation of the world are clearly seen, being understood by the things that are made, even his eternal power and Godhead; so that they are without excuse: Because that, when they knew God, they glorified him not as God, neither were thankful; but became vain in their imaginations, and their foolish heart was darkened.

Professing themselves to be wise, they became fools, And changed the glory of the incorruptible God into an image made like to corruptible man, and to birds, and four footed beasts, and creeping things.

Wherefore God also gave them up to uncleanness through the lusts of their own hearts, to dishonor their own bodies between themselves: Who changed the truth of God into a lie, and worshiped and served the creature more than the Creator, who is blessed for ever. Amen.

For this cause God gave them up unto vile affections: for even their women did change the natural use into that which is against nature:

And likewise also the men, leaving the natural use of the woman, burned in their lust one toward another; men with men working that which is unseemly, and receiving in themselves that recompence of their error which was meet.

And even as they did not like to retain God in their knowledge, God gave them over to a reprobate mind, to do those things which are not convenient; Being filled with all unrighteousness, fornication, wickedness, covetousness, maliciousness; full of envy, murder, debate, deceit, malignity; whisperers, Backbiters, haters of God, despiteful, proud, boasters, inventors of evil things, disobedient to parents, Without understanding, covenant breakers, without natural affection, implacable, unmerciful: Who knowing the judgment of God, that they which commit such things are worthy of death, not only do the same, but have pleasure in them that do them.

Prayer Against Cultural Influence

Father in the name of Jesus we bind the influence of demonic culture. I refuse to conform to society norms that are contrary to the holiness of my Father, Jehovah God.

I activate godly living with holiness as the only standard. I choose to live righteously in the name of Jesus Christ.

I bind and rebuke all demonic mind blinding spirits and spirits of deception in the name of Jesus Christ. I reject all forms of homosexuality, perversion and uncleanliness. I bind these from operating in my body.

Every evil spirit that has enter my life as a result of malestation, incest, rape, sodomy, rejection. I command you to go now in the mighty name of Jesus Christ.

I forgive all who have trespassed against me. I release myself from bitterness, unforgiveness, fear and condemnation in the name of Jesus Christ. Lord Jesus I ask you to shine the light of your glory upon every mental trigger, memory and hidden place that may harbor demonic activities and patterns.

Father God I ask now for a blood bath, wash me in the blood of Jesus Christ. I receive my freedom and liberty through the blood of Jesus Christ and my righteousness is of Christ Jesus. I am a new creature and I am made new ... I am a new woman(man).

Chapter 4
Spiritual Weapons
Prayer Artillery
Higher Levels of Prayer
For
End Time Strategic Warfare

(For the weapons of our warfare are not carnal, but mighty through God to the pulling down of strong holds;)
Casting down imaginations, and every high thing that exalteth itself against the knowledge of God, and bringing into captivity every thought to the obedience of Christ;
2 Corinthians 10:4-5

Releasing the Blood Of Jesus

Prayer
Father God in heaven I receive the finished work of Calvary where Jesus Christ shed his blood. I receive the benefits of the new covenant through Jesus Christ. I am a partaker of the blood of Jesus Christ through the holy communion I eat the Lord's body and drink His precious blood.

The power of sin has been defeated through the blood. Father in heaven let the door post of my body,my home, my family, my life, my ministry, church and community be covered and protected by the blood of Jesus Christ. Father in heaven let me be blood bathed and washed from all unrighteousness. Cleanse my physical body, five senses, soul and spirit in the mighty name of Jesus Christ. I thank you that through the blood I have overcome the devil and the kingdom of darkness.

Prayer

 I now decree and declare deliverance through the blood from sickness and disease, lack and poverty, guilt, shame, condemnation. Father in heaven let the blood of Jesus Christ be a rebuke to every spirit of accusation and slander against me name in Jesus Christ mighty name.

Hebrews 9:14

How much more shall the blood of Christ, who through the eternal Spirit offered himself without spot to God, purge your conscience from dead works to serve the living God?
Hebrews 10:19-20

Having therefore, brethren, boldness to enter into the holiest by the blood of Jesus, By a new and living way, which he hath consecrated for us, through the veil, that is to say, his flesh;

Hebrews 12:24

And to Jesus the mediator of the new covenant, and to the blood of sprinkling, that speaketh better things than that of Abel.

Hebrews 13:20-21

Now the God of peace, that brought again from the dead our Lord Jesus, that great shepherd of the sheep, through the blood of the everlasting covenant, Make you perfect in every good work to do his will, working in you that which is well pleasing in his sight, through Jesus Christ; to whom be glory for ever and ever. Amen.

John 6:54

Whoso eateth my flesh, and drinketh my blood, hath eternal life; and I will raise him up at the last day.

1 John 1:7

But if we walk in the light, as he is in the light, we have fellowship one with another, and the blood of Jesus Christ his Son cleanseth us from all sin.

Matthew 26:25-28

And as they were eating, Jesus took bread, and blessed it, and brake it, and gave it to the disciples, and said, Take, eat; this is my body. And he took the cup, and gave thanks, and gave it to them, saying, Drink ye all of it; For this is my blood of the new testament, which is shed for many for the remission of sins.

Revelation 12:10-11

And I heard a loud voice saying in heaven, Now is come salvation, and strength, and the kingdom of our God, and the power of his Christ: for the accuser of our brethren is cast down, which accused them before our God day and night. And they overcame him by the blood of the Lamb, and by the word of their testimony; and they loved not their lives unto the death.

1 Peter 1:2
Elect according to the foreknowledge of God the Father, through sanctification of the Spirit, unto obedience and sprinkling of the blood of Jesus Christ: Grace unto you, and peace, be multiplied.

Spiritual Weapons

Shield
Ephesians 6:16
above all, taking the shield of faith, wherewith ye shall be able to quench all the fiery darts of the wicked.

Psalms 3:3
But thou, O Lord, art a shield for me; my glory, and the lifter up of mine head.

Shade
Psalms 121:5
The LORD is thy keeper: **the LORD** is thy **shade** upon thy right hand

Authority

We have been given power over all devils according to Matthew 10:1 we also have authority to tread upon serpents and scorpions. Not some power, not a little power but all power of the enemy and that nothing shall by any means hurt us Luke 10:19. Hallelujah!! Praise God Jehovah forever!

The bible tells us that we are seated in heavenly places, this means we have been given a seat of authority through Jesus Christ to govern in the spirit realm. We must be ever mindful of who we are and the authority given against the kingdom of darkness.

Prayer of Rightful Authority

I take my seat of authority in the name of Jesus Christ. I am seated in heavenly places far above all principalities, powers, might and dominion. I clothe myself in the armor of the Lord.

I use the sword of the Spirit which is the word of God to slay powers of darkness. Let every program be destroyed by holy fire that would operate against me through the moon, sun, stars, planets and constellations in the name of Jesus Christ. Father in the name of Jesus rebuke and bind all deities and demonic powers of the sun and the moon.

Psalms 121:6-8

The sun shall not smite thee by day, Nor the moon by night. The LORD shall preserve thee from all evil: He shall preserve thy soul. The LORD shall preserve thy going out and thy coming in From this time forth, and even for evermore.

I Bind the workings of all moon witches and the use of moon water. I release the fire of God to destroy all curses, hexes, vexes and spells. In the name of Jesus I command the moon water to evaporate and dry up now!

The sun shall not smite me by day nor the moon by night the Lord God Almighty shall preserve my soul and redeem my feet from destruction. Let every blessing and spiritual gift that was taken, stolen and hidden be restored now! In Jesus Christ name

Deuteronomy 33:28
Israel then shall dwell in safety alone: the fountain of Jacob shall be upon a land of corn and wine; also his heavens shall drop down dew.

Malichi 3:10
Bring ye all the tithes into the storehouse, that there may be meat in mine house, and prove me now herewith, saith the LORD of hosts, if I will not open you the windows of heaven, and pour you out a blessing, that there shall not be room enough to receive it.

Daniel 10:12-13
Then said he unto me, Fear not, Daniel: for from the first day that thou didst set thine heart to understand, and to chasten thyself before thy God, thy words were heard, and I am come for thy words. But the prince of the kingdom of Persia withstood me one and twenty days: but, lo, Michael, one of the

chief princes, came to help me; and I remained there with the kings of Persia.

Ephesians 1:3
Blessed be the God and Father of our Lord Jesus Christ, who hath blessed us with all spiritual blessings in heavenly places in Christ:

Psalms 18:3
I will call upon the Lord, who is worthy to be praised: so shall I be saved from mine enemies.

Psalms 121:5-7
The Lord is thy keeper: the Lord is thy shade upon thy right hand. The sun shall not smite thee by day, nor the moon by night. The Lord shall preserve thee from all evil: he shall preserve thy soul.

Fire of God
Psalms 97:3
A fire goeth before him, and burneth up his enemies roundabout

Prayer
Father you are enthroned forever there is not a weapon mighty enough to fight against you Jehovah God. For a fire goes before you and burns up your enemies round about Psalms 97:3. Who can stand on the day your fire is released? You Lord have made me a minister of fire and I use the fire to

burn demonic powers in the name of Jesus Christ. God
Jehovah you are great forever! The power of your voice is
heard in the city; show lightning down your arm with the
indignation of his anger and with a flame of devouring fire,
with scattering, tempest and hailstones Isaiah 30:30. Your
lightning scatters enemies Psalms 144:6. *Cast forth lightning,
and scatter them: shoot out thine arrows, and destroy them.* I
am delivered by your fire...Lord God almighty your fire
protects me.

Exodus 14:24
And it came to pass, that in the morning watch the LORD
looked unto the host of the Egyptians through the pillar of fire
and of the cloud, and troubled the host of the Egyptians,

Hebrews 1:7
And of the angels he saith, Who maketh his angels spirits, and
his ministers a flame of fire.

Psalms 18:13
The LORD also thundered in the heavens, and the Highest gave
his voice; hailstones and coals of fire.

Psalms 106:18
And a fire was kindled in their company; the flame burned up
the wicked.

Isaiah 10:17
And the light of Israel shall be for a fire, and his Holy One for
a flame: and it shall burn and devour his thorns and his briers
in one day;

Isaiah 66:15
For, behold, the LORD will come with fire, and with his chariots
like a whirlwind, to render his anger with fury, and his rebuke
with flames of fire.

Psalms 140:10
Let burning coals fall upon them: let them be cast into the fire;
into deep pits, that they rise not up again.

Luke 3:16
John answered, saying unto them all, I indeed baptize you
with water; but one mightier than I cometh, the latchet of
whose shoes I am not worthy to unloose: he shall baptize you
with the Holy Ghost and with fire:

Daniel 7:9
I beheld till the thrones were cast down, and the Ancient of
days did sit, whose garment was white as snow, and the hair of
his head like the pure wool: his throne was like the fiery flame,
and his wheels as burning fire.

Genesis 19:24
Then the LORD rained upon Sodom and upon Gomorrah
brimstone and fire from the LORD out of heaven

Revelation 11:4-5
These are the two olive trees, and the two candlesticks standing before the God of the earth. And if any man will hurt them, fire proceedeth out of their mouth, and devoureth their enemies: and if any man will hurt them, he must in this manner be killed.

Spoilers
Hosea 10:2
Their heart is divided; now shall they be found faulty: he shall break down their altars, he shall spoil their images.

Prayer
Father in heaven according to your word Exodus 15:3 you are a man of war. I employ all necessary weapons with angelic warrior assistance to aid in the battle. Father in heaven, we thank you that you have spoiled the plans of our enemy Satan and the kingdom of darkness.

Ezekiel 39:10
So that they shall take no wood out of the field, neither cut down any out of the forests; for they shall burn the weapons with fire: and they shall spoil those that spoiled them, and rob those that robbed them, saith the Lord GOD.

Collossians 2:15
And having spoiled principalities and powers, he made a shew of them openly, triumphing over them in it.

Luke 11:22
But when a stronger than he shall come upon him, and overcome him, he taketh from him all his armor wherein he trusted, and divideth his spoils.

Job 12:19
He leadeth princes away spoiled, and overthroweth the mighty.

Zechariah 11:3
There is a voice of the howling of the shepherds; for their glory is spoiled: a voice of the roaring of young lions; for the pride of Jordan is spoiled.

1 Samuel 17:53
And the children of Israel returned from chasing after the Philistines, and they spoiled their tents.

War Club

Prayer

Father God I present myself as your war club and weapon of war in the earth I destroy, break into pieces the plans and agendas of witches, warlocks, satanists, sorcerers, psychics and mystics in the name of Jesus Christ. Father God, I ask that you blow up all walls of protection around them. I ask for the fire and the blood of Jesus to render powerless and destroy hexes, vexes, spells, charms. I bind and destroy silver cords and ley lines, projections and command that all demonic portals be closed now in Jesus Christ name.

I release the fire of the living God and the blood of Jesus to destroy the power of jinx, bewitchments, sudden destruction, death, sickness, pain, torments, incense and candle burning, prayer chains, chanting, incantations, hoodoo, JuJu, crystals and Eggs being targeted against myself, my family, ministry and church in Jesus Christ name.

Jeremiah 23:29
Is not my word like as a fire? saith the LORD; and like a hammer that breaketh the rock in pieces?

Judges 4:21
For there are certain men crept in unawares, who were before of old ordained to this condemnation, ungodly men, turning the grace of our God into lasciviousness, and denying the only Lord God, and our Lord Jesus Christ.

Psalms 74:6
A man was famous according as he had lifted up axes upon the thick trees. But now they break down the carved work thereof at once with axes and hammers.

Arm of the Lord

Prayer

Father God, I thank you that you have favored me and Your right hand brings me into my inherited blessings and possession. Let Your arm Father God be against my enemies in the name of Jesus Christ let Your arm establish me for evermore.

Luke 1:51

He hath shewed strength with his arm; he hath scattered the proud in the imagination of their hearts.

Isaiah 51:9

Awake, awake, put on strength, O arm of the LORD; awake, as in the ancient days, in the generations of old. Art thou not it that hath cut Rahab, and wounded the dragon?

Psalms 98:1

O sing unto the LORD a new song; for he hath done marvelous things: his right hand, and his holy arm, hath gotten him the victory.

Job 40:9

Hast thou an arm like God? or canst thou thunder with a voice like him.

Exodus 6:6

Wherefore say unto the children of Israel, I am the Lord, and I will bring you out from under the burdens of the Egyptians, and I will rid you out of their bondage, and I will redeem you with a stretched out arm, and with great judgments:

Psalms 89:10

Thou hast broken Rahab in pieces, as one that is slain; thou hast scattered thine enemies with thy strong arm.

Habakkuk 3:4

And his brightness was as the light; he had horns coming out of his hand: and there was the hiding of his power

Isaiah 52:10

The Lord hath made bare his holy arm in the eyes of all the nations; and all the ends of the earth shall see the salvation of our God.

Chapter 5

Spirit of Sorcery and Witchcraft
Prayer Artillery
Higher Levels of Prayer
For
End Time Strategic Warfare

He disappoints the devices of the crafty so that their hands cannot perform their enterprise.
Job 5:12

Prayer

Father God, I ask that you cover my head on the day of battle. Father in the name of Jesus Christ I bind and break all evil affecting my body, muscular, reproductive, digestive, excretory, circulatory, respiratory and nervous systems.

I command all demons to leave now! In Jesus Christ name... Let all evil powers operating the four elements of the earth: water, wind, fire and earth be destroyed in Jesus Christ mighty name. I bind in the name of Jesus all evil affecting the seven points of the body through witchcraft: the heart, navel, spine, spleen, head, between the eyes and throat in Jesus Christ name.

I return all witchcraft and demons back to the sender according to Psalms 109:17-19 *As he loved cursing, so let it come unto him: as he delighted not in blessing, so let it be far from him. As he clothed himself with cursing like as with his garment, so let it come into his bowels like water, and like oil into his bones. Let it be unto him as the garment which covereth him, and for a girdle wherewith he is girded continually.*

Prayer Against Witchcraft

Father God let their powers be sealed up within themselves so that they become inoperable against anyone else.

I bind and forbid the transference of evil spirits. I sever every ungodly soul tie to people, places or things. Let the invisible cord that binds soul ties be destroyed forever in Jesus Christ Name. I repent of all known and unknown sin. I receive the blood of Jesus Christ as protection against evil forces from the kingdom of darkness in the name of Jesus Christ.

Let them that love their curses receive their curses hundredfold upon their heads in the name of Jesus Christ. Let every witch, warlock and sorcerer be uncovered and stripped of the protecting cloak let no witch, warlock or sorcerer prosper in my presence in the name of Jesus Christ.

I release the love and virtue of Jesus Christ onto every witch or warlock targeting my area of influence and peace may find repentance in the hope of their souls being saved from eternal destruction. In the mighty name of Jesus Christ

Isaiah 54:17

No weapon that is formed against thee shall prosper; and every tongue that shall rise against thee in judgment thou shalt condemn. This is the heritage of the servants of the LORD, and their righteousness is of me, saith the LORD.

1 John 4:4

Ye are of God, little children, and have overcome them: because greater is he that is in you, than he that is in the world.

Galatians 3:13

Christ hath redeemed us from the curse of the law, being made a curse for us: for it is written, Cursed is everyone that hangeth on a tree:

Proverbs 26:2

As the bird by wandering, as the swallow by flying, so the curse causeless shall not come.

Psalms 109:17-19

As he loved cursing, so let it come unto him: as he delighted not in blessing, so let it be far from him.

As he clothed himself with cursing like as with his garment, so let it come into his bowels like water, and like oil into his

Psalms 91:5

He that dwelleth in the secret place of the most High shall abide under the shadow of the Almighty.

*I will say of the L*ORD*, He is my refuge and my fortress: my God; in him will I trust.*

Surely he shall deliver thee from the snare of the fowler, and from the noisome pestilence.

He shall cover thee with his feathers, and under his wings shalt thou trust: his truth shall be thy shield and buckler.

Thou shalt not be afraid for the terror by night; nor for the arrow that flieth by day;

Nor for the pestilence that walketh in darkness; nor for the destruction that wasteth at noonday.

A thousand shall fall at thy side, and ten thousand at thy right hand; but it shall not come nigh thee.

Only with thine eyes shalt thou behold and see the reward of the wicked.

*Because thou hast made the L*ORD*, which is my refuge, even the most High, thy habitation;*

There shall no evil befall thee, neither shall any plague come nigh thy dwelling.

For he shall give his angels charge over thee, to keep thee in all thy ways.

They shall bear thee up in their hands, lest thou dash thy foot against a stone.

Thou shalt tread upon the lion and adder: the young lion and the dragon shalt thou trample under feet.

Because he hath set his love upon me, therefore will I deliver him: I will set him on high, because he hath known my name.

He shall call upon me, and I will answer him: I will be with him in trouble; I will deliver him, and honor him.

With long life will I satisfy him, and shew him my salvation.

Prayer

I am not afraid of the terror by night. I bind demonic interference through dream visitations and bumps in the night. Father in heaven release the glory realm in my night dwelling place. Set your holy angels against spirits of astral projection and covens of witches and sorcerers that seek to invade. Draw a blood line around my home. In Jesus Christ might name.

Matthew 5:44

But I say unto you, Love your enemies, bless them that curse you, do good to them that hate you, and pray for them which despitefully use you, and persecute you;

2 Chronicles 34:24
Thus saith the LORD, Behold, I will bring evil upon this place, and upon the inhabitants thereof, even all the curses that are written in the book which they have read before the king of Judah:

Nehamiah 13:2
Because they met not the children of Israel with bread and with water, but hired Balaam against them, that he should curse them: howbeit our God turned the curse into a blessing.

Prayer Against Evil Cauldrons
Let evil witches cauldron be overturned in the name of Jesus Christ. I decree that the witch and warlocks will drink the brew of their cauldron. Let the witches broom be burned by holy fire in the name of Jesus Christ.

Job 41:20
Out of his nostrils goeth smoke, as out of a seething pot or caldron.

Ezekiel 11:11-12
This city shall not be your caldron, neither shall ye be the flesh in the midst thereof; but I will judge you in the border of Israel: And ye shall know that I am the LORD: for ye have not walked in my statutes, neither executed my judgments, but have done after the manners of the heathen that are round about you.

Jeremiah 1:13-14

And the word of the LORD came unto me the second time, saying, What seest thou? And I said, I see a seething pot; and the face thereof is toward the north. Then the LORD said unto me, Out of the north an evil shall break forth upon all the inhabitants of the land.

Micah 3:3

Who also eat the flesh of my people, and flay their skin from off them; and they break their bones, and chop them in pieces, as for the pot, and as flesh within the caldron.

Prayer Against Spirit Cages

Father God, erase every invisible line that has been drawn around my life and the life of my family and church. Let every demonic container collide with the mighty rock of ages I overcome every snare laid aside for me in the name of Jesus Christ. I am free from every mental cage, my mind is free, my brain is free.

Let every spiritual cage be destroyed and receive fire now in the name of Jesus. Father in heaven release from any cage all mind blockages and memory loss. My mind is blessed. I have the mind of Christ Jesus. Father in heaven let all the blessings you have for me find me give me this day my daily bread and all that you have purposed for this day in Jesus Christ name.

Isaiah 26:4

Trust ye in the Lord for ever: for in the Lord Jehovah is everlasting strength:

Exodus 33:12

And Moses said unto the Lord, See, thou sayest unto me, Bring up this people: and thou hast not let me know whom thou wilt send with me. Yet thou hast said, I know thee by name, and thou hast also found grace in my sight

Exodus 34:7

Keeping mercy for thousands, forgiving iniquity and transgression and sin, and that will by no means clear the guilty; visiting the iniquity of the fathers upon the children, and upon the children's children, unto the third and to the fourth generation.

1 Corinthians 10:13

There hath no temptation taken you but such as is common to man: but God is faithful, who will not suffer you to be tempted above that ye are able; but will with the temptation also make a way to escape, that ye may be able to bear it.

Prayer of Elevation

Father God in heaven let every agent of shame in my life receive fire, every power that comes to steal promotion receive fire, spirit of Pisgah at the edge of breakthrough receive fire, arrows fired against my head receive fire and burn up in the name of Jesus Christ. I reject the spirit of the tail. I am the head and I stand above my counterparts in the name of Jesus Christ. I shall mount up on eagle wings everything I lay my hands to prosper in the name of Jesus Christ. Father God, Joseph was promoted from the pit, remember me and promote my cause. Father in heaven make me your candidate for divine promotion. I receive the anointing by faith to excel in the name of Jesus Christ.

1 Samuel 2:7
The LORD maketh poor, and maketh rich: he bringeth low, and lifteth up.

Psalms 75:6-7
For promotion cometh neither from the east, nor from the west, nor from the south. But God is the judge: he putteth down one, and setteth up another.

Isaiah 40:30-31
Even the youths shall faint and be weary, and the young men shall utterly fall: But they that wait upon the LORD shall renew their strength; they shall mount up with wings as eagles; they shall run, and not be weary; and they shall walk, and not faint

Deuteronomy 15:10
Thou shalt surely give him, and thine heart shall not be grieved when thou givest unto him: because that for this thing the LORD thy God shall bless thee in all thy works, and in all that thou puttest thine hand unto

Prayer Against Barrenness

I bind all spiritual barrenness promoting an agenda against conception in my life, home, marriage, family, ministry and church. Father in heaven I ask that the counter movement of the Holy Spirit to frustrate all evil devices in the name of Jesus Christ.

Father in heaven let the glory of success be a rebuke to every spiritual Peninnah in the name of Jesus Christ. I cry aloud as Hannah did that any barrenness be removed let the Zoe life of God breakforth.

1 Samuel 1:10-17

And she was in bitterness of soul, and prayed unto the Lord, and wept sore. And she vowed a vow, and said, O Lord of hosts, if thou wilt indeed look on the affliction of thine handmaid, and remember me, and not forget thine handmaid, but wilt give unto thine handmaid a man child, then I will give him unto the Lord all the days of his life, and there shall no razor come upon his head. And it came to pass, as she continued praying before the Lord, that Eli marked her mouth.

Now Hannah, she spake in her heart; only her lips moved, but her voice was not heard: therefore Eli thought she had been drunken. And Eli said unto her, How long wilt thou be drunken? put away thy wine from thee.

And Hannah answered and said, No, my lord, I am a woman of a sorrowful spirit: I have drunk neither wine nor strong drink, but have poured out my soul before the LORD.

Count not thine handmaid for a daughter of Belial: for out of the abundance of my complaint and grief have I spoken hitherto. Then Eli answered and said, Go in peace: and the God of Israel grant thee thy petition that thou hast asked of him.

Judges 13:3
And the angel of the LORD said unto Manoah, Of all that I said unto the woman let her beware.

Luke 1:30-31
And the angel said unto her, Fear not, Mary: for thou hast found favor with God. And, behold, thou shalt conceive in thy womb, and bring forth a son, and shalt call his name Jesus.

Prayer For Children
Father God in heaven I ask that you will pour your Holy Spirit upon (name) give (name) the grace to develop a heart for the righteousness of God. May they forever walk in your ways and be skilled and knowledgeable of Your holy word. Close their hearts from the ever present evils in the world let them discern between right and wrong. Cause their obedience to dismantle demonic devices.

I pray that (name) will not be blasphemers of the Holy Spirit. Loose them from pride, foolery, anxiety, broken heart and rebellion.
I ask Father God that they will grow in revelation, wisdom, understanding and discernment in the name of Jesus Christ.

Father in the name of Jesus Christ, keep (name) from all sexual pollution and sexual lust (name) cause (name) to resist the devil. Let (name) be mindful that they are the temple of the Holy Ghost.

Holy Spirit I ask that you would convict (insert) of pornography, masturbation, adultery and fornication. I pray in the name of Jesus Christ that (name) will walk in the spirit so as not to fulfill the lust of the flesh in the mighty name of Jesus Christ.

I ask that (name) would walk in wholeness and restoration of body, soul and spirit. Give them supernatural grace to forgive others who may have trespassed against them. Remove from (name) and every yolk and fellowship of ungodly wisdom and counsel. Loose from their soul and spirit gateways traumas and experience.

Loose from them the spirit of victimization through rape and sodomy and bind victory to them in the name of Jesus Christ. In the name of Jesus Christ I bind mental illness and traumas linked to chemical imbalances. I bind depression, addictions, suicide, anger, self harm and murder I command all these spirits to go now in the name of Jesus Christ.

Father God I ask that you would cause (name) to understand the purpose for which they were created. Let wisdom lead in all decision making concerning finances. I ask that (name) will be gainfully employed. That they will give into the kingdom of God in support of God's work on earth.

I release the word of Psalms 91 as the banner over (name). Psalms 91:1-16 *He that dwelleth in the secret place of the most High shall abide under the shadow of the Almighty.*

I will say of the LORD, He is my refuge and my fortress: my God; in him will I trust.

Surely he shall deliver thee from the snare of the fowler, and from the noisome pestilence.

He shall cover thee with his feathers, and under his wings shalt thou trust: his truth shall be thy shield and buckler.

Thou shalt not be afraid for the terror by night; nor for the arrow that flieth by day;

Nor for the pestilence that walketh in darkness; nor for the destruction that wasteth at noonday.

A thousand shall fall at thy side, and ten thousand at thy right hand; but it shall not come nigh thee.

Only with thine eyes shalt thou behold and see the reward of the wicked.

Because thou hast made the LORD, which is my refuge, even the most High, thy habitation;

There shall no evil befall thee, neither shall any plague come nigh thy dwelling.

For he shall give his angels charge over thee, to keep thee in all thy ways.

They shall bear thee up in their hands, lest thou dash thy foot against a stone.

Thou shalt tread upon the lion and adder: the young lion and the dragon shalt thou trample under feet.

Because he hath set his love upon me, therefore will I deliver him: I will set him on high, because he hath known my name.

He shall call upon me, and I will answer him: I will be with him in trouble; I will deliver him, and honor him.

With long life will I satisfy him, and shew him my salvation.

Let the protection of the blood of Jesus Christ shield me from every attack. In the name of Jesus Christ I speak health, wealth and wholeness into my body I bind sickness and disease.

I bind Galatians 5:22-23 *(But the fruit of the Spirit is love, joy, peace, longsuffering, gentleness, goodness, faith, Meekness, temperance: against such there is no law.)*

Upon (name) in the name of Jesus Christ. Bind the spirit of suicide, self harm, self hate and crimes against others in the name of Jesus Christ. Lord Jesus Christ please bring comfort to (name). Let (name) experience your love and presence in this moment. Thank you Lord Jesus

Proverbs 22:6
Train up a child in the way he should go: and when he is old, he will not depart from it.

Colossians 3:20
Children, obey your parents in all things: for this is well pleasing unto the Lord.

Ephesians 4:29
Let no corrupt communication proceed out of your mouth, but that which is good to the use of edifying, that it may minister grace unto the hearers.

Ephesians 4:32
And be ye kind one to another, tenderhearted, forgiving one another, even as God for Christ's sake hath forgiven you.

Proverbs 13:20
He that walketh with wise men shall be wise: but a companion of fools shall be destroyed.

Proverbs 15:5
A fool despiseth his father's instruction: but he that regardeth reproof is prudent.

Proverbs 20:11
Even a child is known by his doings, whether his work be pure, and whether it be right.

Jeremiah 29:11
For I know the thoughts that I think toward you, saith the LORD, thoughts of peace, and not of evil, to give you an expected end.

John 3:16
For God so loved the world, that he gave his only begotten Son, that whosoever believeth in him should not perish, but have everlasting life.

Matthew 19:14
For God so loved the world, that he gave his only begotten Son, that whosoever believeth in him should not perish, but have everlasting life.

1 Timothy 4:12
Let no man despise thy youth; but be thou an example of the believers, in word, in conversation, in charity, in spirit, in faith, in purity.

Matthew 18:10
Take heed that ye despise not one of these little ones; for I say unto you, That in heaven their angels do always behold the face of my Father which is in heaven

Chapter 6
Covenants and Contracts
Prayer Artillery
Higher Levels of Prayer
For
End Time Strategic Warfare

Hannah Made a Vow
And she vowed a vow, and said, O LORD of hosts, if thou wilt indeed look on the affliction of thine handmaid, and remember me, and not forget thine handmaid, but wilt give unto thine handmaid a man child, then I will give him unto the LORD all the days of his life, and there shall no razor come upon his head. 1 Samuel 1:11

Matthew 11:12
And from the days of John the Baptist until now the kingdom of heaven suffereth violence, and the violent take it by force.

Matthew 18:18
Verily I say unto you, Whatsoever ye shall bind on earth shall be bound in heaven: and whatsoever ye shall loose on earth shall be loosed in heaven.

Judges 2:1
And an angel of the LORD came up from Gilgal to Bochim, and said, I made you to go up out of Egypt, and have brought

you unto the land which I sware unto your fathers; and I said, I will never break my covenant with you.

Mark 14:24
And he said unto them, This is my blood of the new testament, which is shed for many.

Isaiah 54:17
No weapon that is formed against thee shall prosper; and every tongue *that* shall rise against thee in judgment thou shalt condemn. This *is* the heritage of the servants of the LORD, and their righteousness *is* of me, saith the LORD.

<u>Blood Covenants</u>
Leviticus 17:10-12
And whatsoever man *there be* of the house of Israel, or of the strangers that sojourn among you, that eateth any manner of blood; I will even set my face against that soul that eateth blood, and will cut him off from among his people.

Prayer Against Food Covenants And Contracts

I Bind... Partaking in food or beverages in waking life or in dreams that are demonic initiations, I rebuke and reject receiving peculiar money in waking life or in dreams. Father God I ask now that all ancestral agreements be destroyed by the blood of Jesus Christ.

I bind all power from cursed objects spiritual and natural...rabbit's foot, rings, necklaces, moon water etc;

I rebuke all witchcraft initiation, and spiritual initiation done with or without my knowledge. Holy Spirit I ask you to reveal things in my home or around my life that may have ties to the kingdom of darkness.

Deliverance

Moses was used to deliver the children of Israel from bondage in Egypt. The Egyptians did not want to let the people of Israel go. It is important to seek deliverance; it is also equally important to remain free not to enter into bondage again. We must obey the work of God for our lives.

Prayer of Deliverance

I speak to every stubborn spirit that refuses to let go and release me out of bondage. I command you to be dismantled in the name of Jesus Christ. I receive deliverance from all captivity and all oppression in the name of Jesus Christ. The Lord God is my deliverer, Lord you will free me from evil oppressors.

For You have come to set the captive free.
Luke 4:18 *The Spirit of the Lord is upon me, because he hath anointed me to preach the gospel to the poor; he hath sent me to heal the brokenhearted, to preach deliverance to the*

captives, and recovering of sight to the blind, to set at liberty
them that are bruised,

Thank You My Lord and Savior

Romans 6:14-19
for sin shall not have dominion over you: for ye are not under the law, but under grace. What then? shall we sin, because we are not under the law, but under grace? God forbid. Know ye not, that to whom ye yield yourselves servants to obey, his servants ye are to whom ye obey; whether of sin unto death, or of obedience unto righteousness?

But God be thanked, that ye were the servants of sin, but ye have obeyed from the heart that form of doctrine which was delivered to you.

John 8:36
If the Son therefore shall make you free, ye shall be free indeed.

Numbers 20:16
And when we cried unto the LORD, he heard our voice, and sent an angel, and hath brought us forth out of Egypt:
and, behold, we *are* in Kadesh, a city in the uttermost of thy border:

Psalms 34:17

The righteous cry, and the LORD heareth, and delivereth them out of all their troubles.

Galatians 5:1

Stand fast therefore in the liberty wherewith Christ hath made us free, and be not entangled again with the yoke of bondage.

Psalms 50:15

And call upon me in the day of trouble: I will deliver thee, and thou shalt glorify me

2 Samuel 22:2

And he said, The LORD is my rock, and my fortress, and my deliverer;

Judges 6:8-10

That the LORD sent a prophet unto the children of Israel, which said unto them, Thus saith the LORD God of Israel, I brought you up from Egypt, and brought you forth out of the house of bondage;

1 Samuel 17:45

Then said David to the Philistine, Thou comest to me with a sword, and with a spear, and with a shield: but I come to thee in the name of the LORD of hosts, the God of the armies of Israel, whom thou hast defied.

Prayer Against Captivity

Father God I thank you for deliverance free me from all oppressors, humble every spiritual Pharoah, cause the land of spiritual Egypt's representing a place of captivity receive your judgments. Rebuke every stubborn spirit of lack, sickness, disease, fear, complacency, slavery and bondage which refuses to let us go! Father lead the enemies against my soul to the place where x marks the spot and drown each spirit in the Red Sea. In the name of Jesus Christ. Let there arise the spirit of Moses within that I may be led to all the promises that you have ascribed for my life.

We decree and declare let my
People
Go!

Wherefore he saith, When he ascended up on high, he led captivity captive, and gave gifts unto men. Ephesians 4:8

Direction

***For I know the thoughts that I think toward you,
saith the L<small>ORD</small>, thoughts of peace, and not of evil, to
give you an expected end
Jeremiah 29:11***

There are very pivotal points in our lives in which we must desperately hear the voice of God for directions. We are vehicles in the earth by which God uses to carry out His agenda. Like with most vehicles today they come equipped with internal GPS systems for drivers to utilize. Most people use the GPS when they are not familiar with where they are going and that makes good sense.

It would be considered not wise to drive somewhere you have never been and you are not aware how to get there. Why? Simply, because you would end up lost... Well the same is likely concerning our spiritual lives if we don't use the GPS [God's Positioning System] we are likely to get lost and end up on a road God never intended us to travel on. And face delays, accidents, and vehicle malfunctions.

Many times the GPS system seems as though it is taking you out of the way but in all actuality it is mapping the best route for your travels helping to avert traffic delays, accidents and road construction. God is doing the same for us mapping out a plan to help avert things that would hinder us on our journey. He says in His word Jeremiah 29:11-13 *For I know the thoughts that I think toward you, saith the* LORD, *thoughts of peace, and not of evil, to give you an expected end. Then shall ye call upon me, and ye shall go and pray unto me, and I will hearken unto you. And ye shall seek me, and find me, when ye shall search for me with all your heart.*

It is important that when we are not sure about the way the GPS [God's Positioning System] is leading us that we continue to trust in His directions to make our ETA [estimated time of arrival]. Father in heaven thank you for leading and guiding my feet in the way You would have for me to go. Psalms 37:23-24 *The steps of a good man are ordered by the LORD: And he delighteth in his way. Though he fall, he shall not be utterly cast down: For the LORD upholdeth him with his hand.*

Prayer of Direction

I reject inner rebellion against the leading of the Holy Spirit. I rebuke the contrary, leading through voices that are not of you. Your sheep hear your voice. I will only respond to your voice and follow You. My spiritual compass is set on the word of God.

Psalms 119:105 Thy word is a lamp unto my feet, and a light unto my path. I am eternally yours through the blood of Jesus at the cross of Calvary and nothing and no one will ever be able to pluck me out of your hands neither take me away from divine destiny in Jesus Christ name.

John 10:27-28
My sheep hear my voice, and I know them, and they follow me: And I give unto them eternal life; and they shall never perish, neither shall any man pluck them out of my hand.

Proverbs 3:5-6
Trust in the Lord with all thine heart; and lean not unto thine own understanding. In all thy ways acknowledge him, and he shall direct thy paths

Psalms 37:23-24
The steps of a good man are ordered by the Lord: and he delighteth in his way. Though he fall, he shall not be utterly cast down: for the Lord upholdeth him with his hand

Psalms 32:8
I will instruct thee and teach thee in the way which thou shalt go: I will guide thee with mine eye

Jeremiah 29:11
For I know the thoughts that I think toward you, saith the Lord, thoughts of peace, and not of evil, to give you an expected end.

Isaiah 48:17-18
Thus saith the Lord, thy Redeemer, the Holy One of Israel; I am the Lord thy God which teacheth thee to profit, which leadeth thee by the way that thou shouldest go.

O that thou hadst hearkened to my commandments! then had thy peace been as a river, and thy righteousness as the waves of the sea

Favor

Comfort ye, comfort ye my people, saith your God. Speak ye comfortably to Jerusalem, and cry unto her, that her warfare is accomplished, that her iniquity is pardoned: for she hath received of the LORD's hand double for all her sins. Isaiah 40:2

Arise, shine; for thy light is come, and the glory of the LORD is risen upon thee.
Isaiah 60:1

Prayer of Favor
Lord, I thank you that the set time of favor has come upon my life. I receive your divine favor that will cause a flow of wealth and influence to fulfill your purpose for my life. I thank you Father in heaven that your favor is causing a great exodus from a place of lack and financial captivity and bondage. Father God, your favor will stop tragedy and calamities from forming in my life in the name of Jesus Christ.

Lord God release your favor and make me wealthy and whole and double my health, wealth and financial worth in times of famine. Lord God crown my head with favor and grace to reap your harvest in the mighty name of Jesus Christ.

Psalms 102:13
Thou shalt arise, and have mercy upon Zion: for the time to favor her, yea, the set time, is come

Proverbs 16:7
When a man's ways please the LORD, he maketh even his enemies to be at peace with him.

Fear

Fear thou not; for I am with thee: be not dismayed; for I am thy God: I will strengthen thee; yea, I will help thee; yea, I will uphold thee with the right hand of my righteousness.
Isaiah 41:10

Prayer Against Fear
Father God I thank you, You have not given me the spirit of fear I walk in perfect love. I rebuke the spirit of fear in the name of Jesus Christ. I put my total trust in you, my Lord. I will not fear what man can do to me. I may walk through the valley of the shadow of death but I have no cause to fear for God is always by my side.

Father in heaven I know you have not planned any defeat for me, every thought that you think towards me is good. You have a desire for my destiny to come into complete manifestation. Your banner over me Lord God is love and I receive victory over fear!

Psalms 23:4
Yea, though I walk through the valley of the shadow of death, I will fear no evil: for thou art with me; thy rod and thy staff they comfort me.

1 John 4:18
There is no fear in love; but perfect love casteth out fear: because fear hath torment. He that feareth is not made perfect in love.

Phillippians 4:6-7
Be careful for nothing; but in every thing by prayer and supplication with thanksgiving let your requests be made known unto God. And the peace of God, which passeth all understanding, shall keep your hearts and minds through Christ Jesus

2 Timothy 1:7
For God hath not given us the spirit of fear; but of power, and of love, and of a sound mind.

Isaiah 41:10

Fear thou not; for I am with thee: be not dismayed; for I am thy God: I will strengthen thee; yea, I will help thee; yea, I will uphold thee with the right hand of my righteousness.

Proverbs 29:25

The fear of man bringeth a snare: but whoso putteth his trust in the LORD shall be safe.

Jeremiah 29:11

For I know the thoughts that I think toward you, saith the LORD, thoughts of peace, and not of evil, to give you an expected end

Psalms 27:1-3

A Psalm of David. The LORD *is* my light and my salvation; whom shall I fear? the LORD *is* the strength of my life; of whom shall I be afraid?
When the wicked, *even* mine enemies and my foes, came upon me to eat up my flesh, they stumbled and fell. Though an host should encamp against me, my heart shall not fear: though war should rise against me, in this *will* I *be* confident.

Gates

Lift up your heads, O ye gates; and be ye lift up, ye everlasting doors; and the King of glory shall come in. Who is this King of glory? The LORD strong and mighty, the LORD mighty in battle. Lift up your

heads, O ye gates; even lift them up, ye everlasting doors; and the King of glory shall come in. Who is this King of glory? The LORD *of hosts, he is the King of glory. Selah. Psalms 24:7-10*

Prayer Against Demonic Gates

Father God, thank you that the gates of hell shall not prevail against my life. I am your temple of the Holy Ghost. Matthew 16:18 *And I say also unto thee, That thou art Peter, and upon this rock I will build my church; and the gates of hell shall not prevail against it.* Lord God let every gate be open for the King of Glory to possess in my life.

I receive treasures of darkness and hidden riches in secret places in Jesus name. Isaiah 45:3 *And I will give thee the treasures of darkness, and hidden riches of secret places, that thou mayest know that I, the* LORD, *which call thee by thy name, am the God of Israel.*

In the mighty name of Jesus Christ I possess the gates of my enemies. I release battering rams against every satanic gate holding my possessions. I sound the trumpet in the spirit realm arise apostolic gate keepers, prophetic gatekeepers, evangelistic gatekeepers take your positions in Jesus Christ's mighty name.

Wage an effective warfare and possess the city. Let every gate that has been broken by demonic devices be repaired in the name of Jesus Christ.

Prayer to Open Spiritual Gates

I command my eye gate to see prophetically, I command my ear gate to hear what the Lord is saying by the Holy Spirit, I command my mouth gate to say what the Lord is saying and release words of wisdom, understanding and prophecy. I command my eye, ear and mouthgate to be holy in the name of Jesus Christ. Lord God re-establish the gates of praise and worship in my life.

Isaiah 45:1-3

Thus saith the Lord to his anointed, to Cyrus, whose right hand I have holden, to subdue nations before him; and I will loose the loins of kings, to open before him the two leaved gates; and the gates shall not be shut; I will go before thee, and make the crooked places straight: I will break in pieces the gates of brass, and cut in sunder the bars of iron: And I will give thee the treasures of darkness, and hidden riches of secret places, that thou mayest know that I, the Lord, which call thee by thy name, am the God of Israel.

Psalms 118:9

It is better to trust in the Lord than to put confidence in princes.

Ezekiel 21:22

At his right hand was the divination for Jerusalem, to appoint captains, to open the mouth in the slaughter, to lift up the voice with shouting, to appoint battering rams against the gates, to cast a mount, and to build a fort.

Isaiah 60:18

Violence shall no more be heard in thy land, wasting nor destruction within thy borders; but thou shalt call thy walls Salvation, and thy gates Praise.

Isaiah 60:11

Therefore thy gates shall be open continually; they shall not be shut day nor night; that men may bring unto thee the forces of the Gentiles, and that their kings may be brought.

Genesis 28:17

And he was afraid, and said, How dreadful is this place! this is none other but the house of God, and this is the gate of heaven.

Oh Mighty, Mighty Gates of Brass and Gates of Iron Be Opened
In the Mighty Name of Jesus Christ

Chapter 7
Governments & Nations
Prayer Artillery
Higher Levels of Prayer
For
End Time Strategic Warfare

For unto us a child is born, unto us a son is given: and the government shall be upon his shoulder: and his name shall be called Wonderful, Counsellor, The mighty God, The everlasting Father, The Prince of Peace Isaiah 9:6

Prayer Over Governments

Lord Jesus Christ you are Lord of Lords, your kingdom reigns supreme forever. Righteousness and justice belong to You. Let your kingdom come on earth as it is in heaven regarding my city, state and nation. Let the earthly governments surrender to your authority, Lord Jesus release a consuming fire and burn up the idols of the city.

In the name of Jesus Christ I bind the theft in the city, let every synagogue of satan's seat be removed and cast down from local government to national governments. Father God in heaven command all the prince rulers of our cities, states to be removed and bound and their ruling scepters removed, crush their demonic diadems under the weight of your glory and let their seats be destroyed in the mighty name of Jesus Christ.

Prayer of Awakening

Father God I ask for a great awakening and release of the five-fold ministers of fire to redeem the harvest. Let your mighty sickle be in their hands to reap the spoils and souls that are captive by principalities and rulers of darkness. Father God, in heaven punish the prince rulers in our nation with Your power, trample them under foot and make an open show of your glory in the name of Jesus Christ.

Lord reveal and expose demonic vices and schemes, expose all secret entry points into our nation housing human trafficking. Set the captive free Lord Jesus Christ. Lord Jesus spoil these principalities operating in the FDA, educational sector, financial sector, healthcare sector, entertainment and agriculture sector.

Psalms 76:12
He shall cut off the spirit of princes: he is terrible to the kings of the earth.

Matthew 6:10
Thy kingdom come, Thy will be done on earth, as it is in heaven.

Colossians 2:14-15
Blotting out the handwriting of ordinances that was against us, which was contrary to us, and took it out of the way, nailing it to his cross; And having spoiled principalities and

powers, he made a shew of them openly, triumphing over them in it.

Joshua 13:21
And all the cities of the plain, and all the kingdom of Sihon king of the Amorites, which reigned in Heshbon, whom Moses smote with the princes of Midian, Evi, and Rekem, and Zur, and Hur, and Reba, which were dukes of Sihon, dwelling in the country.

Nations

Let every soul be subject unto the higher powers. For there is no power but of God: the powers that be are ordained of God. Whosoever therefore resisteth the power, resisteth the ordinance of God: and they that resist shall receive to themselves damnation.
Romans 13:1-2

Prayer for Nations
Father you said in Your word that If my people, which are called by my name, shall humble themselves, and pray, and seek my face, and turn from their wicked ways; then will I hear from heaven, and will forgive their sin, and will heal their land. Lord, I cry out to you on behalf of my nation, save us from calamity and destruction. Lord help us to seek your face and live. Help us to desire righteousness over wickness.

Proverbs 14:34

Righteousness exalts a nation, but sin is a reproach to any people

Prayer of National Restoration

Lord it is Your righteousness that lifts and restores nations. I ask that my nation will remember your righteousness and Your holiness. Help those who govern in my nation to rule in the fear of the Lord.

Remove those who oppose righteousness according to Your word. Expose every satanic agenda, disallow the promotion and the workings of sin in my nation and break the power of electoral schemes, lies and deception.

Father in heaven let your justice reign from the north to the south and from the east to the west. I ask for divine angelic assistance to bind every demonic king and prince seated in governmental positions.

Father in heaven I ask you to overturn laws and ordinances that were instituted to promote premature judgment for my nation. Father in the name of Jesus Christ protect my nation from all countries that seek to invade my nation, secretly.

Expose all secret conversation and plans to bring nuclear and bio chemical warfare and destruction to my nation's land. Awaken the body of believers and the watchmen to stand on the walls of prayer to intercede and to intercept spiritual devices of Satan in the name of Jesus Christ.

I pray that we, your people, will humble ourselves from all forms of pride, idolatry and spiritual adultery and seek earnestly your face and your righteousness and turn from sin and repent of our iniquity. We know that you will hear our cries and our prayers.

Heal our land and remove the wicked from ruling and being appointed in our governmental offices. Bring godly fear to those who make laws governing the people in Jesus Christ name. Bring godly unity to our nation according to Mark 3:24-26 a kingdom divided can not stand.

Ezra 10:14
Let now our rulers of all the congregation stand, and let all them which have taken strange wives in our cities come at appointed times, and with them the elders of every city, and the judges thereof, until the fierce wrath of our God for this matter be turned from us.

Psalms 2:2-4
The kings of the earth set themselves, and the rulers take counsel together, against the LORD, and against his anointed, *saying*, Let us break their bands asunder, and cast away their cords from us. He that sitteth in the heavens shall laugh: the Lord shall have them in derision.

Isaiah 14:4-6

And it shall come to pass in the day that the LORD shall give thee rest from thy sorrow, and from thy fear, and from the hard bondage wherein thou wast made to serve, That thou shalt take up this proverb against the king of Babylon, and say, How hath the oppressor ceased! the golden city ceased! The LORD hath broken the staff of the wicked, *and* the scepter of the rulers. He who smote the people in wrath with a continual stroke, he that ruled the nations in anger, is persecuted, *and* none hindereth.

Isaiah 14:12

How art thou fallen from heaven, O Lucifer, son of the morning! *how* art thou cut down to the ground, which didst weaken the nations!

Proverbs 2:1-8

My son, if thou wilt receive my words, and hide my commandments with thee; So that thou incline thine ear unto wisdom, and apply thine heart to understanding; Yea, if thou criest after knowledge, and liftest up thy voice for understanding; If thou seekest her as silver, and searchest for her as for hid treasures; Then shalt thou understand the fear of the LORD, and find the knowledge of God. For the LORD giveth wisdom: out of his mouth cometh knowledge and understanding.

He layeth up sound wisdom for the righteous: he is a buckler to them that walk uprightly. He keepeth the paths of judgment, and preserveth the way of his saints.

Job 12:23-25
He increaseth the nations, and destroyeth them: he enlargeth the nations, and straiteneth them again. He taketh away the heart of the chief of the people of the earth, and causeth them to wander in a wilderness where there is no way. They grope in the dark without light, and he maketh them to stagger like a drunken man.

Proverbs 11:14
Where no counsel is, the people fall: but in the multitude of counselors there is safety.

2 Chronicles 7:14
If my people, which are called by my name, shall humble themselves, and pray, and seek my face, and turn from their wicked ways; then will I hear from heaven, and will forgive their sin, and will heal their land.

Jeremiah 29:7
And seek the peace of the city whither I have caused you to be carried away captives, and pray unto the LORD for it: for in the peace thereof shall ye have peace.

Romans 13:1
Let every soul be subject unto the higher powers. For there is no power but of God: the powers that be are ordained of God

1 Timothy 2:1-2
I exhort therefore, that, first of all, supplications, prayers, intercessions, and giving of thanks, be made for all men; For kings, and for all that are in authority; that we may lead a quiet and peaceable life in all godliness and honesty.

Healing

Many are the afflictions of the righteous: but the LORD delivereth him out of them all. Psalms 34:19

Prayer of Healing
Thank you Lord Jesus Christ for the finished work on the cross. It is by your stripes I am healed. It is through your blood sacrifice that I am made whole. You have made me free from sickness and disease.

I rebuke every spirit of infirmity operating in the members of my body. Every sickness with a name I command you to bow at the name of Jesus Christ now! Call out the spirit(s) that are invading you and command them to go in Jesus Christ name.

Lord arise over me with Your healing wings.

1 Peter 2:24
Who his own self bare our sins in his own body on the tree, that we, being dead to sins, should live unto righteousness: by whose stripes ye were healed.

James 5:14-15
Is any sick among you? let him call for the elders of the church; and let them pray over him, anointing him with oil in the name of the Lord: And the prayer of faith shall save the sick, and the Lord shall raise him up; and if he have committed sins, they shall be forgiven him.

Matthew 10:8
Heal the sick, cleanse the lepers, raise the dead, cast out devils: freely ye have received, freely give.

Jeremiah 17:14
Heal me, O LORD, and I shall be healed; save me, and I shall be saved: for thou art my praise.

Mark 10:52
And Jesus said unto him, Go thy way; thy faith hath made thee whole. And immediately he received his sight, and followed Jesus in the way.

Luke 8:50
But when Jesus heard it, he answered him, saying, Fear not: believe only, and she shall be made whole.

Be Encouraged

Jesus Christ heals the broken heart perhaps your heart is heavy and you are facing depression, grief, anger, betrayal and suicide etc. No matter what it may be, He is a healer, take the opportunity to call up on Him for your deliverance. With confidence knowing that the chastisement of our peace was upon Him.

Psalms 147:3
He healeth the broken in heart, and bindeth up their wounds.

Proverbs 8:13
Keep me as the apple of the eye, hide me under the shadow of thy wings, From the wicked that oppress me, from my deadly enemies, who compass me about. They are enclosed in their own fat: with their mouth they speak proudly.

They have now compassed us in our steps: they have set their eyes bowing down to the earth; Like as a lion that is greedy of his prey, and as it were a young lion lurking in secret places.

Arise, O Lord, disappoint him, cast him down: deliver my soul from the wicked, which is thy sword:

Restoration

And I will restore to you the years that the locust hath eaten, the cankerworm, and the caterpiller, and the palmerworm, my great army which I sent among you.

*And ye shall eat in plenty, and be satisfied, and praise the name of the L*ORD *your God, that hath dealt wondrously with you: and my people shall never be ashamed.*

Joel 2:25-26

It is in the purposes of God that each of His children receive restoration. He was first in instituting restoration to mankind through Jesus Christ. He restored our fellowship and relationship. In the garden of Eden Adam lost the fellowship with God when he and Eve were deceived by the serpent.

But God had formed a plan from the foundations of the world which included His only begotten Son to shed His blood and die on a cross of Calvary for ultimate redemption and restoration.

However, the serpent is yet deceiving, Satan comes to steal, kill and destroy these are his attributes. But like in the garden of Eden when he came to steal from Adam the Lord had a plan of recovery.

And Satan has come to steal from us, but the Lord God has a plan... He said I came that you might have life. Let's look at

John 10:10 *The thief cometh not, but for to steal, and to kill, and to destroy: I am come that they might have life, and that they might have it more abundantly.*

Prayer of Restoration

I bind every demonic theft name of Jesus Christ I receive divine strength to pursue my pursers. Father I ask that you put all my enemies to shame and force them to return and release my possessions and inheritance.

Father God I asked that you would arrest and sentence those responsible for all theft naturally and spiritually. I command every demonic power responsible for theft to give back to me a one hundred fold return on property, health, wealth, gifts, buildings, vehicles, cups, crowns, relationships and ministry.

In the name of Jesus Christ I destroy by a consuming fire all allied confederacies against my life, all persons and personalities who have attempted to steal my identity in the physical and spiritual realms I command you to be embarrassed and put to open shame.

I command all copy-cat crowns, robes, authorities, shoes and garments to be permanently destroyed in the name of Jesus Christ. I stand with the favor of queen Esther and I command every Vashti to remove the crown and seat of favor and authority. Go now to dry places of exile in the mighty name of Jesus Christ.

Father God, send your warring angels on a search and seize mission in the earth and in the waters, to recover those things hidden from me in the kingdom of darkness. In Jesus Christ name

Restoration, Restoration, Restoration, Restoration,
Restoration,
Restoration, Restoration
Now in the Mighty Name of Jesus Christ

Dreams, Visions, Creativity, Witty ideas be restored now!

Genesis 40:13
Yet within three days shall Pharaoh lift up thine head, and restore thee unto thy place: and thou shalt deliver Pharaoh's cup into his hand, after the former manner when thou wast his butler

Leviticus 25:28
But if he be not able to restore it to him, then that which is sold shall remain in the hand of him that hath bought it until the year of jubile: and in the jubile it shall go out, and he shall return unto his possession

Nehemiah 5:12
Then said they, We will restore them, and will require nothing of them; so will we do as thou sayest. Then I called the priests,

and took an oath to them that they should do according to this promise.

Psalms 51:12
Restore unto me the joy of thy salvation; and uphold me with thy free spirit.

Jeremiah 30:17
For I will restore health unto thee, and I will heal thee of thy wounds, saith the LORD; because they called thee an Outcast, saying, This is Zion, whom no man seeketh after.

Judges 2:1
And an angel of the LORD came up from Gilgal to Bochim, and said, I made you to go up out of Egypt, and have brought you unto the land which I sware unto your fathers; and I said, I will never break my covenant with you.

Vindication

Vindicate me, O God, and defend my cause against an ungodly people, from the deceitful and unjust man deliver me. For you are the God in whom I take refuge; why have you rejected me? Why do I go about mourning because of the oppression of the enemy? Send out your light and your truth; let them lead me;
let them bring me to your holy hill and to your dwelling! Then I will go to the altar of God, to God my exceeding joy, and I will praise you with the lyre, Oh God, my God.

Psalms 35:24

Prayer of Vindication
Father God in heaven arise and let your enemies be scattered.

Let your justice vindicate my cause. Let none of my enemies testify against me. But deliver and rescue me from the appetite of them that seek to devour. Let Your wisdom cloak me and provide a way of escape. You provided a way of escape for the children of Israel through the Red Sea. Father in heaven let every spiritual Egyptian drown as they chase me to my promises in the name of Jesus Christ.

Father in the name of Jesus Christ let every spiritual Hamen after my crown and divine place of destiny hang upon the gallows he has prepared for my downfall.

Hamen's Gallows

Esther 7:9-10
And Harbonah, one of the chamberlains, said before the king, Behold also, the gallows fifty cubits high, which Haman had made for Mordecai, who spoken good for the king, standeth in the house of Haman. Then the king said, Hang him thereon. So they hanged Haman on the gallows that he had prepared for Mordecai. Then was the king's wrath pacified.

Psalms 98:2
The Lord hath made known his salvation: his righteousness hath he openly shewed in the sight of the heathen.

Isaiah 58:8
Then shall thy light break forth as the morning, and thine health shall spring forth speedily: and thy righteousness shall go before thee; the glory of the Lord shall be thy reward.

Psalms 35:23
Stir up thyself, and awake to my judgment, even unto my cause, my God and my Lord.

Psalms 82:3
Defend the poor and fatherless: do justice to the afflicted and needy.

Isaiah 54:17
No weapon that is formed against thee shall prosper; and every tongue that shall rise against thee in judgment thou shalt condemn. This is the heritage of the servants of the LORD, and their righteousness is of me, saith the LORD

Luke 18:3
I will call upon the LORD, who is worthy to be praised: so shall I be saved from mine enemies.

Psalms 37:6
And he shall bring forth thy righteousness as the light, and thy judgment as the noonday.

Psalms 7:12-16
God judgeth the righteous, And God is angry with the wicked every day. If he turn not, he will whet his sword; He hath bent his bow, and made it ready

Psalms 72:4
He shall judge the poor of the people, he shall save the children of the needy, and shall break in pieces the oppressor.

Monitoring Spirits
Monitoring spirits also known as familiar spirits are demonic. The monitoring demons and or demonic spirits work in collaboration with witches, warlocks, necromancers and those who practice divination.

These demonic entities are disembodied beings that seek a host to dwell in and communicate with.

As we have read in Matthew 8:32 the devils were cast out of a man into swine. So it is possible for spirits to embody human beings and animals.

Prayer Against Seers
Without Appropriation

Father God I ask that You would send your angels on assignment to bind evil monitoring spirits and ancestral demons. I reject and denounce all practices through heritage and lineage outside of the righteousness of the Living God. I rebuke all seers and watchers of the spirit realm without appropriation that are not sent by Jehovah God in the name of Jesus Christ.

Matthew 8:28-34
And when he was come to the other side into the country of the Gergesenes, there met him two possessed with devils, coming out of the tombs, exceeding fierce, so that no man might pass by that way.

And, behold, they cried out, saying, What have we to do with thee, Jesus, thou Son of God? art thou come hither to torment us before the time? And there was a good way off from them an herd of many swine feeding.

So the devils besought him, saying, If thou cast us out, suffer us to go away into the herd of swine. And he said unto them, Go. And when they were come out, they went into the herd of swine: and, behold, the whole herd of swine ran violently down a steep place into the sea, and perished in the waters.

And they that kept them fled, and went their ways into the city, and told everything, and what was befallen to the possessed of the devils.

And, behold, the whole city came out to meet Jesus: and when they saw him, they besought him that he would depart out of their coasts.

We see in scripture that it is possible for animals to have devils ...
Those who devise wickedness offer animals up in sacrificial ceremonies. Using the bodies of animals every year during October Halloween is celebrated.

It is not uncommon to see Halloween prompts of witches with cats and crows in department stores for those who celebrate to decorate their homes etc. This is not altogether a coincidence; there is a fellowship with the kingdom of darkness and some animals.

But glory be to God no matter what form darkness manifests in we have power over all the power of the enemy.

Read this scripture with me
Luke 10:19
Behold, I give unto you power to tread on serpents and scorpions, and over all the power of the enemy: and nothing shall by any means hurt you.

Do you see that! What a mighty God we serve... nothing or NO - THING shall be any means HURT you!

Prayer

Father God we thank you for the victory that only you can give. I take the authority you have given me to tread upon serpents and scorpions that would try to surround my life. I walk in the full power and authority by which you have ordained and crowned me with. I rebuke and bind every strange spirit, every animalistic spirit. I ask you to send your warring angels to bind all demonically used animals that squawk, bark and purr against my destiny, family, community and church. In the name of Jesus Christ.

8 Prayer Watches

Ecclesiastes 3:1-9

To every thing there is a season, and a time to every purpose under the heaven:

A time to be born, and a time to die; a time to plant, and a time to pluck up that which is planted;

A time to kill, and a time to heal; a time to break down, and a time to build up;

A time to weep, and a time to laugh; a time to mourn, and a time to dance;

A time to cast away stones, and a time to gather stones together; a time to embrace, and a time to refrain from embracing;

A time to get, and a time to lose; a time to keep, and a time to cast away;

A time to rend, and a time to sew; a time to keep silence, and a time to speak;

A time to love, and a time to hate; a time of war, and a time of peace.

What profit hath he that worketh in that wherein he laboureth?

God has set in place times and seasons

that includes every tongue, tribe and nation

God has set in motion seasons and times these 8 prayer watches are quite notable as it relates to scriptures. Each watch has a specific manifestation one we could relate to is the watch in which Paul and Silas praised, sung and worshiped the Lord. And at the midnight hour a mighty quake happened and their prison bars were broken. Setting Paul and Silas free...

And hath made of one blood all nations of men for to dwell on all the face of the earth, and hath determined the times before appointed, and the bounds of their habitation;
Acts 17:26

First Watch
6 pm to 9 pm
Reflect and Meditate on the things of God. This is a quiet fellowship.
Matthew 14:15
And when it was evening, his disciples came to him, saying, This is a desert place, and the time is now past; send the multitude away, that they may go into the villages, and buy themselves victuals.

Second Watch

9 pm to 12 am

A time of intercession this is a time of offensive prayers before the enemy. This is the time to release the judgments of God against satanic devices against the educational system, judicial system, economic, religious and political systems. Psalm 119:62

At midnight I will rise to give thanks to You because of Your righteous judgments.

Third Watch

12 am to 3 am

This is a high demonic activity watch this is a time of spiritual warfare. This is also referred to as the witching hour. In which witches, warlocks and satanism release their curses and spells to carry out demonic assignments.

This is a good time to enter into the presence of the Lord through praise and worship. A good demonstration of this is Paul and Silas: And at midnight Paul and Silas prayed, and sang praises unto God: and the prisoners heard them. And suddenly there was a great earthquake, so that the foundations of the prison were shaken: and immediately all the doors were opened, and every one's bands were loosed. Acts 16:25-34

And at midnight Paul and Silas prayed, and sang praises unto God: and the prisoners heard them.

And suddenly there was a great earthquake, so that the foundations of the prison were shaken: and immediately all the doors were opened, and every one's bands were loosed.

And the keeper of the prison awaking out of his sleep, and seeing the prison doors open, he drew out his sword, and would have killed himself, supposing that the prisoners had been fled.

But Paul cried with a loud voice, saying, Do thyself no harm: for we are all here.
Then he called for a light, and sprang in, and came trembling, and fell down before Paul and Silas, And brought them out, and said, Sirs, what must I do to be saved? And they said, Believe on the Lord Jesus Christ, and thou shalt be saved, and thy house. And they spake unto him the word of the Lord, and to all that were in his house.

Forth Watch
3 am to 6 am
This is the time of divine visitation, and angelic instruction. This is the hour of revelation and illumination. Make your request known to God and command the new day. Early will I seek you Lord.

Fifth Watch
6 am to 9 am
Malachi 4:2-4
Pray that the Holy Spirit will strengthen and cultivate our assignments.

The Lord shall arise with healing in His wings. During this watch pray for the healing of the nation and your body, healing in relationships. Pray for the government, and the economy.

Sixth Watch
9 am to 12 pm
Pray during this watch for the divine harvest includes souls and things pertaining to your peace. Call forth your harvest businesses, finances, salvations etc. During this watch pray for healing and forgiveness releasing others of their trespasses.

Seventh Watch
12 pm to 3 pm
Pray during this watch for deliverance from evil, pray against satanic arrows and destruction against your life and those around you and church ministries.

Eighth Watch
3 pm to 6 pm
Prayer during this watch for the manifestation of the Glory of God!
Revival and the resurrection of dead things. Pray for the church and the body of Christ into proper seasons and times.

Father God in heaven we thank you for every victory and for every triumph. Thank you for every prayer answered. You are a faithful God. Amen!

It is through you, Lord Jesus Christ that
We Have
Victory Over Darkness

To the only wise God our Savior, be glory and majesty, dominion and power, both now and ever. Amen.
Jude 25

Citing:
KJV Biblegateway.com
Mess Biblegateway.com

Made in the USA
Columbia, SC
22 February 2025

54098681R00083